growing **root**
vegetables

growing root
vegetables

**a directory of varieties and how to
cultivate them successfully**

Richard Bird

LORENZ BOOKS

This edition is published by Lorenz Books

Lorenz Books is an imprint of
Anness Publishing Ltd, Hermes House
88–89 Blackfriars Road, London SE1 8HA
tel. 020 7401 2077; fax 020 7633 9499
www.lorenzbooks.com; info@anness.com

© Anness Publishing Ltd 2003

This edition distributed in the UK by
The Manning Partnership Ltd
tel. 01225 478 444; fax 01225 478 440
This edition distributed in the USA and
Canada by National Book Network
tel. 301 459 3366; fax 301 429 5746
This edition distributed in Australia by
Pan Macmillan Australia
tel. 1300 135 113; fax 1300 135 103
This edition distributed in New Zealand
by David Bateman Ltd
tel. (09) 415 7664; fax (09) 415 8892

A CIP catalogue record for this book is
available from the British Library.

Publisher: Joanna Lorenz
Managing Editor: Judith Simons
Project Editor: Felicity Forster
Editor: Lydia Darbyshire
Additional text: Jessica Houdret and
    Susie White
Photographers: Jonathan Buckley,
    John Freeman, Michelle Garrett,
    Andrea Jones, Debbie Patterson and
    Polly Wreford
Jacket photographer: Martin Brigdale
Illustrator: Liz Pepperell
Designer: Paul Calver
Editorial Reader: Penelope Goodare
Production Controller: Darren Price

The material in this book has been previously
published as part of a larger book, *The Kitchen
Garden Book*.

10 9 8 7 6 5 4 3 2 1

Contents

Introduction

The plants encompassed by the expression "root vegetables" are some of the most frequently eaten and most useful of all garden produce. Potatoes, one of the most important food crops in the world, fall into this group, as do carrots and parsnips. The group also includes some less familiar vegetables, such as salsify and scorzonera, and some less often eaten ones, such as Jerusalem artichokes, swedes (rutabagas or yellow turnips) and kohl rabi. All, however, are easy to grow and, in a well-planned garden, can provide fresh produce for the kitchen all year round.

CULTIVATION

Anyone who is interested in what they eat would do well to consider growing their own vegetables. Mounting concerns about the residues of fungicides, pesticides, artificial fertilizers and other chemicals in and on our foods have been intensified by the use of genetically modified crops and the dawning realization that it is almost impossible to know exactly what it is that we are putting in our own mouths and, perhaps more importantly, in the mouths of our children. Growing your own vegetables is the ideal solution.

When you eat carrots and potatoes that you have grown yourself from seed or from plantlets bought from a reputable supplier you know that they are free from all taint of additives. When growing your own vegetables, you can use the minimum of artificial pesticides and fertilizers and time the applications so that you do not eat anything that has been recently sprayed with chemicals.

BELOW It is not difficult to grow your own vegetables. Some hardy crops – including leeks, Brussels sprouts, cabbages and these red-topped turnips – can be left outdoors in autumn and harvested as they are needed.

LEFT Even a small vegetable garden can yield a good crop of potatoes and beetroot (beets).

Root vegetables are some of the most important crops you can grow in your vegetable garden, but unlike some other edible crops, such as herbs and tree fruits, most of them are not particularly decorative. Perhaps only beetroot (beets), with their vivid red leaves, and Jerusalem artichokes, with their bright yellow flowers, are worth growing in the ornamental garden; the rest are best planted in a specially cultivated part of the vegetable garden.

Many root vegetables are, perhaps surprisingly, closely related to the cabbage. Turnips and swedes, for example, are members of the brassica family, as are kohl rabi, and these plants tend to suffer from the same diseases as cabbage. It is important, therefore, that you treat them as cabbages when you are planning the rotation of your vegetable plot so that they are not grown in the same soil in consecutive years.

HARVESTING

All vegetables taste best when they are freshly harvested from the garden, and root vegetables are no exception. One of the advantages of growing vegetables is that you can plan to have crops reaching maturity when you want them. Sowing a number of short rows over several weeks will allow you to enjoy succulent young carrots or crunchy radishes for a far longer period than the few short weeks that the mass-produced equivalent is available in a supermarket.

Freshly harvested root vegetables can also be stored so that they will last through the winter and will take up little space in a frost-proof garage or shed. Even if you do not have room to store lifted vegetables for a month or two, bear in mind that many

RIGHT There are few more satisfying meals than a tasty stew with home-grown potatoes, carrots and turnips.

root vegetables, notably swedes, winter radishes, salsify and scozonera, can be left in the ground and dug up as and when you need them.

COOKING

Few people will need to be convinced of the merits of crunchy radishes or small, juicy carrots. Other root vegetables, however, though normally cooked, can be delicious raw when young and fresh. The unusual, subtly peppery taste of kohl rabi will enhance salads, while the cooked roots taste wonderful on their own or as an addition to a casserole. Parsnips, swedes and turnips are traditional ingredients in hearty, warming soups and stews, but the fresh roots, lifted from your own garden, will have a flavour and texture far different from the woody, tasteless produce available in supermarkets and will encourage you to experiment with dishes so that you can enjoy them to the full.

types of
root
vegetable

The expression "root vegetable" is used to describe an enormous range of plants, but all have in common the fact that the edible part develops entirely or partially below ground. These vegetables range from those such as beetroot (beets) that take up little space and can even be grown in a flower bed or border to those such as potatoes, swedes and turnips that will do best in a dedicated vegetable plot. All, however, are well worth growing and produce nutritious and flavourful vegetables that can be used in a wide range of dishes.

Beetroot *Beta vulgaris*

Closely related to Swiss chard, beetroot (beet) has a distinctive bright red coloration. This is not only manifest in the leaves and stems of the plant but also in the roots themselves, and when they are cut or bruised they exude a wonderfully deep red juice. When it is cooked, the flesh is still a very deep colour, even though it loses a lot of colour in the water if it is boiled (baking preserves it). Not everyone likes this coloration – it tends to stain not only other food, but lips and clothes as well.

However, although you never see them in greengrocers, there are also white and golden varieties, which are equally delicious but do not cause the staining. There are also a few fancy ones in which the roots are made up of concentric rings of white and red flesh. The general shape is round or near round, but cylindrical and even tapered varieties are available.

The green or reddish-green leaves can also be eaten when they are young, either in salads or cooked like spinach.

Unlike parsnips and carrots, the bulk of the vegetable's swollen root sits on top of the ground so that you can watch its development and easily determine when it is ready to harvest.

HISTORY

Beetroot originated around the shores of the Mediterranean and was spread northwards into the rest of Europe by the Romans. Once the Romans reached northern and eastern Europe, the vegetable seems to have been taken to heart, and many of the recipes in use today come from these areas. By the mid-19th century it was clearly a popular vegetable, and in her famous cookbook Mrs Beeton has 11 recipes for it, including beetroot fritters and a beetroot and carrot jam.

VARIETIES

One of the drawbacks of the older varieties was their tendency to bolt (produce a flower shoot at the expense of the root), especially if

white beetroot

purple beetroot

golden beetroot

ABOVE Most forms of beetroot have spherical roots and red stalks.

they were sown early in the year. Selective hybridization has meant that there are now plenty of named varieties that do not have this characteristic, and one of the best known of these is 'Boltardy' (globe), which is reliable even when sown early.

Another aspect of choosing varieties is related to germination. Most seed is, in fact, made up of a cluster of seeds, which means that when they germinate they produce several seedlings close together. If they are to develop well, the seedlings should be thinned, but this can be a fiddly and time-consuming task, so you might want to look out for what are known as monogerm varieties, which usually have the word "mono" somewhere in their name. 'Monogram' (globe) is a vigorous plant, with smooth skin and rich red roots. 'Moneta' (globe) and 'Cheltenham Mono'

(globe) have the additional advantage of being resistant to bolting.

Varieties with roots of different colours have also been developed. The globe 'Albina Vereduna' ('Snow White') has pale skin and white flesh. The Italian 'Chioggia Pink' (globe) has concentric circles of pink and white, although these disappear on cooking, as the flesh turns to soft pink. The golden-yellow roots of 'Burpee's Golden' (globe), another bolt-resistant form, retain their colour even when cooked; the tops are excellent steamed or boiled, and the roots store well. The oval roots of 'Red Ace' are a deep rich red; this is a strong grower that will do well even in dry seasons.

Also worth trying are two decorative forms, with handsome red leaves that are a valuable addition to salads; these are 'Bull's Blood' and 'McGregor's Favourite'.

NUTRITION

Beetroot has long been considered medicinally beneficial and is recommended as a general tonic. It can be used to help disorders of the blood, including anaemia, it is an effective detoxifier and, because of its high fibre content, it is recommended to relieve constipation. Beetroot contains calcium, iron and vitamins A and C – all at their highest levels when it is eaten raw. The leaves, which have the flavour of spinach, are high in vitamins A and C, and they also contain more iron and calcium than spinach itself.

PREPARING AND COOKING

Remove the leaves by twisting them off, 3–5cm/1–2in from the root. This prevents the beetroot (beets) losing their colour by "bleeding" when they are cooked.

To bake in the oven, place the cleaned beetroot in a dish with a tight-fitting lid, and add about 60–75ml/4–5 tbsp of water. Lay a double layer of foil over the dish before covering with the lid, then bake in a low oven for 2–3 hours or until the beetroot is tender.

Check occasionally to ensure the dish doesn't dry out and to see whether the beetroot is cooked. It is ready when the skin begins to wrinkle and can be easily rubbed away with your fingers.

Alternatively, simply wrap the beetroot in a double layer of foil and bake in a low oven until tender. To boil beetroot, prepare as above and simmer the whole roots for about 1½ hours.

Once cooked, beetroot can be blended to a purée in a food processor. This is an essential ingredient of the classic Russian and Polish soup, borscht.

Turnips *Brassica napa* Rapifera Group

Members of the cabbage family, turnips are closely related to swedes – so closely, in fact, that their names are often confused. For instance, swedes are often called Swedish turnips or swede-turnips, and in Scotland swedes are known as neeps, a varation of the word turnip.

The Western form of the turnip is round, sometimes an almost perfect globe, sometimes slightly flattened. It has one thickish root or several roots emerging from the base. The skins are a creamy white, and the top of the globe can be green, purple, white or creamy yellow. The flesh is white or yellowish. As it grows, the globe is partly sunk into the ground, but most of it is above ground. In Asia long-rooted varieties are also grown, and seed of this form is sometimes available in the West.

green-topped turnips

It is also possible to find old European varieties with long roots.

The fleshy ball is cooked and eaten, and many gardeners also enjoy the young leaves, which are cooked as spring greens. Summer turnips are succulent and can be used in a range of dishes. Those that are overwintered are not quite as tender, but are useful in casseroles, stews and soups. In Japan they are often eaten raw.

HISTORY

The origins of the turnip go back so far that they are obscure, but the wild plant from which it is derived is still commonly found throughout Europe and Asia and is thought to have been cultivated as far back as prehistoric times. The long history has meant that many forms have appeared in cultivation, particularly

LEFT These turnips – a variety known as 'Tokyo Cross' – have just been harvested and will grace any dining table.

in China and Japan. The popularity of the turnip has waned in the West, and with it the number of different forms, although some 30 varieties are available.

Until recently, turnips have not enjoyed a high reputation among cooks in many parts of the world. This is partly because they are perceived as cattle food and partly because few people have taken the trouble to find acceptable ways of cooking them. Schools and other institutions tend to boil and then mash them to a watery pulp, and this is the only way many people have eaten the vegetable.

The French, unlike the British, have always respected the turnip. For centuries they have devised recipes for their delicate navets, roasting them, caramelizing them in sugar and butter or simply steaming and serving with butter. Young, tender turnips have also been popular all over the Mediterranean region for many years, and there are many dishes using turnips with fish or poultry, or teamed with tomatoes, onions and spinach.

VARIETIES

Turnips are generally green or white, although purple, reddish and even black forms have been grown in the past and are sometimes available through specialist seed merchants.

Among the older varieties that can still be found is the maincrop 'Golden Ball', which, as the name suggests, produces round, yellow-tinged roots; it has some resistance to bolting. Another bolt-resistant variety is 'Atlantic', which has purplish tops. 'Veitch's Red Globe' has red tops but white roots, which store well in the ground; this is a good choice for areas with a fairly short growing season. 'Green Scotch Top', with yellow flesh and green shoulders, also keeps well in the ground. The young roots of the early 'Snowball' have a delicious sweet flavour, and a good all-season variety is 'Tokyo Cross', which can be sown at any time from late spring to early autumn. The unusual 'Black Sugarsweet' has a long root with sweet white flesh; these turnips store well over winter. 'Oasis', a new virus-resistant variety,

RIGHT Small, round navets (left) have a sweeter taste than ordinary turnips (right).

produces small, white, round roots with a sweet, juicy flavour.

French navets, which are small, round, rather squashed-looking turnips tinged with pink or purple, are becoming increasingly widely available and are worth seeking out. Even more highly prized by the French are the long, carrot-shaped turnips, known as vertus, which are tender and sweet.

NUTRITION

This cruciferous vegetable is said to halt the onset of certain cancers, particularly rectal cancer. It is also a digestive and maintains bowel regularity. Turnips are a good source of calcium and potassium. The green tops are rich in beta carotene and vitamin C.

PREPARING AND COOKING

Young turnips should not need peeling; simply trim, then simmer or steam until tender. They are delicious raw, thinly sliced or grated into salads.

Peel older turnips and then slice or dice before cooking. To avoid rankness, blanch old turnips if they are to be served as a vegetable dish, or add sparingly to soups and casseroles, so that the flavour is dispersed throughout.

Swedes *Brassica napus* Napobrassica Group

One of those vegetables that never seem to be included in ready-prepared, convenience dishes, swedes (rutabagas or yellow turnips) are popular with cooks who prepare their own food. They belong, perhaps, more to what one might call the category of "wholesome food" (such as stews) than to high cuisine, but they are increasingly used in a wide range of dishes, including delicate soups. Swedes could also be seen as convenience food – it takes only a matter of seconds to pull one from the ground, peel, chop and put it to cook.

Like a number of other root vegetables, swedes actually belong to the cabbage family, as the appearance of the foliage clearly reveals. As such, they tend to suffer from the same pests and diseases as cabbages, and for this reason should be included with that vegetable when you are planning a rotational system.

Swedes generally have a more substantial, rounder flavour than turnips, although fresh young roots have a subtle, pleasant taste. The swollen root mainly develops above ground, with just a small proportion buried in the earth. The flesh is usually a creamy yellow, which deepens during cooking. The roots can be left in the ground for several months unless the weather is exceptionally cold, although it is usually best to lift the early-maturing varieties, which can become rather tough and woody if they are left in the ground for too long.

Many gardeners used to sow a late crop of swedes, around midsummer, to provide the leaves – known as "tops" – which can be used as greens in spring. When they are grown for this purpose, plants can be closer together than those intended for conventional use.

PREPARING AND COOKING

Peel swedes and then cut them into even-sized chunks.

Swedes are delicious when boiled together with carrots and turnips. They should be tender, but take care not to overcook them – check frequently while they cook.

VARIETIES

'Acme Purple Top'
'Best of All'
'Brora'
'Devon Champion'
'Lizzie'
'Marian'
'Ruby'
'Western Perfection'

HISTORY

Swedes are not very old as vegetables go, although no one is certain about their origins. It seems likely that they appeared in Europe as a random cross between turnips and cabbages at some time in the Middle Ages. They did not find their way to Britain until the latter part of the 18th century, and it is thought that they were introduced from Sweden, hence the name. The American name rutabaga also has

purple-topped swedes

Swedish origins, being derived from the word *rotbagga*, which is Swedish for "ram's foot", an apt visual description of a small or immature swede's slender growth.

VARIETIES

The top of the globe – usually known as the shoulder – of the better garden varieties is usually purple, while the lower section, which is hidden from the light, is white. However, yellow swedes with shoulders of various colours have been developed.

One of the most reliable and widely grown swedes is 'Best of All', which has white flesh. 'Marian' (sometimes sold as 'Marianne'), a yellow-fleshed variety with a distinctive flavour, has some resistance to powdery mildew and to club root, as does 'Joan', which is a good selection for early sowing and tends not to split. 'Acme Purple Top' (sometimes listed simply as 'Acme') produces medium-sized roots. 'Merrick', which has white flesh, has a turnip-like flavour. 'Sharpe's Yellow Garden' is a reliable, yellow-fleshed form.

Older varieties, which generally have more flavour and tend to be hardier than more recent introductions, include 'Champion Purple Top', a large, purple-topped swede with orange-yellow, globe-shaped roots. The round, mid-season 'Devon Champion', which also has orange-yellow flesh and purple shoulders, has an excellent flavour. Among the traditional European varieties that are sometimes available from specialist suppliers are the small, white-fleshed 'Bjursas' (from Sweden) and 'Bangholm Fenix' (from Denmark), which produces red-topped orange to purplish roots with a good flavour; these will store well even when lifted.

NUTRITION

Like other members of the brassica family, swedes contain compounds that are believed to have antioxidant properties. They are also thought to be useful in reducing the risk of cancer. They are a good source of vitamins A and C and contain traces of vitamins B1 and B2. They also supply potassium and calcium.

cut swedes

Kohl rabi *Brassica oleracea* Gongylodes Group

Although it is not strictly a root vegetable because it grows above ground, kohl rabi is included in this group because of its similarity to the turnip. In reality, it is a short-stemmed cabbage, but the stem is swollen into a round ball. The fact that it is a stem can be seen from the cabbage-like leaves that sprout out from all around the swelling, unlike those of a turnip, which grow on top. The skin is either green or purple, depending on variety, and the flesh is white. Because it is a stem, kohl rabi sits on or just above the ground, with a taproot descending into the soil.

Kohl rabi has a fresh, mildly peppery taste, which is somewhat similar to that of turnips, and it is useful in a wide range of dishes, including soups, as well as being eaten as a vegetable in its own right. It can also be eaten raw – in salads, for example. From the gardener's point of view it has an advantage over the turnip in that it can be grown in drier conditions yet still retain its succulence. Most varieties should be harvested while they are still quite small – about the size of a tennis ball – but some varieties, such as 'Gigante', which comes from the Czech Republic, usually grow to 4.5kg/10lb or more but remain succulent.

white-skinned
kohl rabi

HISTORY

This curious vegetable is a relative newcomer to gardens, and it is thought to have originated in Europe as late as the 15th or 16th century, although it may have developed earlier – Pliny describes a similar type of vegetable being grown by the Romans in the 1st century AD. No matter when it originated, kohl rabi is not as popular today as it should be. Even after four centuries it is still something of a rarity in France, Britain and the United States, although it is more widely grown in Germany and Austria – as is testified by varieties such as 'Purple Vienna' and 'White Vienna' – as well as in eastern Europe.

LEFT This is a perfect specimen of kohl rabi, which is ready for harvesting. It is delicious both raw and cooked, in a wide range of dishes.

'Cindy', and 'Logo', which produces bulbs no more than about 5cm/2in across, is useful in a small garden.

NUTRITION

Kohl rabi is a cruciferous vegetable packed with phytochemicals, which numerous studies have shown can reduce the risk of various forms of cancer. Phytochemicals are a group of compounds found in varying amounts in all fruit and vegetables, but particularly in cruciferous vegetables. Their compounds include carotenoids, selenium, fibre, isothiocyanates, indoles, phenols, tocopherols, bioflavonoids and protease inhibitors.

VARIETIES

Kohl rabi seed is often sold simply as purple or green forms, but there are many named varieties to choose among, all with the same fresh, slightly peppery flavour, which has been likened to the taste of water chestnuts. The purple-skinned varieties tend to be slightly hardier than the white-skinned ones, which will be a consideration if you live in an area with penetrating winter frosts or a short growing season.

One of the most popular of the purple-skinned varieties is 'Purple Danube', which has an exceptionally sweet flavour and good colour. It can be eaten raw, as a colourful addition to a salad, or cooked. It has the additional advantage of keeping well without becoming woody. The traditional purple-skinned variety 'Purple Vienna' has white flesh and can be harvested until early winter. The slightly earlier 'White Vienna'

(sometimes known as 'Green Vienna') has creamy-white, mild-tasting flesh, which can be grated for adding to salads or cooked in soups and stews.

The heritage variety 'Gigante' (also called 'Gigante Winter') is worth growing if you can find a supplier. Although it grows so large, the white flesh remains crisp and well flavoured and does not become woody and tough, even in storage. The leafy tops are a valuable source of winter greens.

'Blusta', a comparatively recent introduction, produces vivid purple-to blue-skinned bulbs with white flesh, which has a sweet, rather nutty flavour; this variety has some resistance to becoming woody, which can be a problem if bulbs are allowed to grow too large.

Another purple-skinned variety, 'Azur Star', matures quickly and has tasty leaves. 'Quick Star', a fast-growing form, has green-skinned bulbs. An early-maturing variety is

PREPARING AND COOKING

Peel the kohl rabi, slice them unless very small, then boil or steam until just tender. Serve with butter or a creamy sauce. If they are any bigger than 5cm/2in in diameter, they can be stuffed. To do this, hollow out a little before cooking and stuff with fried onions and tomatoes, place in a baking dish with a little water and bake in a medium oven. They can also be cooked slowly in gratin dishes.

Carrots *Daucus carota*

Many people may wonder if it is worth growing carrots when they are so cheap to buy. The answer must be an emphatic "yes". Fresh carrots, whether old or young, that are taken straight from the ground before being cooked taste infinitely better than shop-bought ones: there is no comparison. You may have to put up with them being covered in mud and perhaps with slug and carrot fly holes in them, but this is a minor drawback compared with the superior taste.

The edible part of the carrot develops below ground, while above are the attractive filigree leaves. Although mainly grown for the kitchen, they are well worth growing as purely decorative plants.

HISTORY

Wild carrots can be found throughout Europe and well into Asia. The exact origin of domestic carrots is rather obscure, but they probably originated in the countries of the eastern Mediterranean, and possibly even in Afghanistan. The original domesticated ones were various colours, including white, yellow, purple and red, and carrots of these colours are currently being hybridized and will soon be re-introduced by seed merchants. The orange ones, with which we are all familiar, were developed in Holland and France at a much later date.

VARIETIES

Carrots bought in supermarkets tend to look the same, but there are dozens of named varieties to choose from, including earlies and maincrop to give you a crop over a long period, as well as different shapes and colours, which suit different growing conditions. 'Early Nantes' is a quick-maturing carrot, with good, rich orange roots. The fairly new early 'Jeannette' (a Nantes-type carrot) produces smooth, conical roots, which are equally tasty raw and cooked; the leafy

freshly harvested carrots with their green, feathery tops

tops make pulling easy. 'Fly Away' and 'Sytan' show good resistance to carrot root fly. The deep orange roots of 'Ingot', which are excellent raw or cooked, have good levels of vitamin C and beta carotene.

Among the round-rooted varieties are 'Early French Frame' and 'Parmex', both earlies and both producing tender, bite-sized carrots. 'Parmex' is a particularly good choice for stony soil, as is 'Early French Frame', which produces little, round, golf-ball-sized roots. 'Parabel' and 'Rondo' are fast-maturing carrots, with small, round roots.

Maincrop varieties include the reliable 'Autumn King', which has large, well-coloured roots that can be safely left in the ground and will not split, even in frost. 'Bertan' has also been developed so that the roots

do not split if left in the ground. If your soil is very sandy, the quick-growing 'Boston' is worth trying. As the name suggests, 'Jumbo' will grow very large but still remain tasty. One of the best of the traditional maincrop varieties is 'James Scarlet Intermediate', which produces roots to about 12cm/5in long; they store well once lifted.

Coloured carrots include 'Yellowstone', which has long, smooth, canary-yellow roots with a delicious sweet flavour. The yellow roots of 'Jaune du Doubs', a traditional French variety, are useful for inclusion in stews and soups; it is suitable for growing on shallow soil and stores well in winter. 'White Belgium', another old variety, is not hardy but the white roots are very tasty.

The recently introduced 'Healthmaster' is said to contain 30 per cent more beta carotene than other carrots. It is a maincrop variety, producing roots to 20–25cm/8–10in long.

ABOVE There are few more delicious vegetables than freshly harvested carrots.

NUTRITION

A single carrot will supply enough vitamin A for an entire day, and carrots also contain high levels of the antioxidant beta carotene; antioxidants are widely believed to help reduce the risk of cancer, as well as possibly aiding recovery from it. Carrots also contain useful amounts of vitamins B3, C and E. When eaten raw, they provide good quantities of potassium, calcium, iron and zinc, but these are reduced when carrots are boiled.

The idea that carrots are good for your night sight originated in World War II. Early radar stations were established along the coast of England in 1939 to detect air or sea aggressors. The Germans attributed this sudden remarkable night vision to the British habit of eating carrots. However, vitamin A does indeed form retinol, a lack of which causes night blindness.

PREPARING AND COOKING

Carrots are excellent cooked or raw. Children often like raw carrots, which have a sweet flavour. They can be cut into julienne strips, with a dressing added, or grated into salads and coleslaw – their juices blend with the dressing. As an accompaniment, cut them into julienne strips and braise in butter and dry (hard) cider, or cook in stock and toss in butter and a spinkling of caraway seeds.

To steam carrots, place them over a pan of boiling water for 2–4 minutes until just tender.

Purée carrots in a food processor or blender until smooth, adding a little water if necessary. Pour back into a clean pan and reheat gently, to make a wonderfully rich soup.

Jerusalem artichokes
Helianthus tuberosus

Surprisingly, these potato-like tubers are grown on plants that are closely related to the decorative sunflower. Unlike the dinner-plate-sized flowers of its relative, however, the flowers of the Jerusalem artichoke are small, although they are borne on equally tall stems. The knobbly tubers are found below ground, and they can be used as a vegetable and cooked in the same way as potatoes or parsnips – roasting is a particularly good way of cooking them. They have a pleasantly distinct flavour eaten on their own and also combine well in other dishes, especially soups. Up to about the size of an egg, they are good cooked whole or eaten raw; larger ones are best cut in pieces and cooked.

This is a very easy vegetable to grow. It is not particular about the soil and is troubled by few pests

smooth Jerusalem artichokes

and diseases. The only significant problem is getting rid of it if you decide to stop growing it at any stage. A single piece of one of the tubers that is left in the ground will resprout to produce a new plant, and it is, unfortunately, easy to miss one or more pieces as you dig them up. The regrowth normally appears in the row, however, and plants will not

VARIETIES

Often listed simply as
Jerusalem artichokes.
'Boston Red'
'Dwarf Sunray'
'Fuseau'

spread throughout the garden unless you are careless enough to distribute the tubers about.

Although Jerusalem artichokes are grown primarily as a vegetable, they can also be used to provide a temporary windbreak. They grow rapidly, sometimes to heights of 3m/10ft, and make a dense hedge of wiry stems that needs no additional support except in exposed sites.

The mature plants make excellent windbreaks within the kitchen garden, as well as creating visual screens that can be used to divide up a large garden.

HISTORY

Jerusalem artichokes have no connection with Jerusalem nor with globe artichokes. They originated in North America, where they were cultivated by Native American Indians as long ago as the 15th century. They were brought to Europe in the 16th century, eventually finding their way to Britain via Holland in the early 17th century. The name Jerusalem is believed to be a corruption of the Italian word for sunflower, *girasole*, or it may be

knobbly Jerusalem artichokes

derived from the name of the town in the southern Netherlands, Terneuzen, from where they were sent to Britain.

VARIETIES

Most often you will find that the tubers of Jerusalem artichokes do not have individual names – indeed, you are more likely to find tubers for planting in the supermarket than in the garden centre. However, in recent years a number of named varieties have been developed and some heritage varieties have been made available, and it is always worth searching out these cultivars in catalogues and garden centres because they have been selected for flavour, reliability, disease resistance or hardiness. One of the most widely grown varieties is 'Fuseau', which has long, smooth tubers that are much easier to prepare for cooking than the traditional knobbly varieties; they have a distinctive, rather smoky taste, which is very good in soups. 'Dwarf Sunray', which often produces the typical sunflower blooms, is a shorter growing form, ideal for windy gardens. It produces numerous side tubers, with tender skin, which means that they do not need peeling.

'Boston Red', a popular cultivar in North America, produces large, knobbly tubers with a purple skin and white flesh. They have a strong, characteristic flavour. 'Patate', one of the older varieties, has large, round, smooth tubers. 'Waldboro Gold' is unusual in having yellow tubers, which are rather long and thin, so they are difficult to prepare, but have an excellent taste.

NUTRITION

The tubers are a good source of vitamin B1 and iron and also contain significant amounts of vitamins B2 and B3, calcium, potassium and fibre. Carbohydrate is present as inulin, a sort of fructose, which is tolerated by people with diabetes and can be used as a substitute for glucose.

PREPARING AND COOKING

The white flesh of Jerusalem artichokes turns purplish-brown when it is exposed to light, so when peeling or slicing them raw, place them in a bowl of acidulated water (water with the juice of about half a lemon added). Because Jerusalem artichokes are so knobbly, it is often easier to boil them in acidulated water in their skins and peel them afterwards – the cooked skins should slip off easily.

Jerusalem artichokes can be cooked in many of the ways in which you would cook potatoes or parsnips. They are excellent roasted, sautéed or dipped in batter and fried, but first par-boil them for 10–15 minutes until nearly tender. For creamed artichokes, mix with potatoes in equal amounts; this slightly blunts their flavour and makes a tasty side dish, which does not overpower other flavours.

BELOW Though their shape makes them awkward to peel, Jerusalem artichokes are well worth growing.

Here, Jerusalem artichokes are being processed with celery and milk to make a creamy soup.

Parsnips *Pastinaca sativa*

There is something rather old-fashioned about parsnips. They conjure up images of cold winter evenings and warm, comforting broths eaten in front of a blazing wood fire. Nowadays parsnips are available all year through, but many people still feel they belong to winter, adding their characteristic flavour to soups and stews.

Parsnips are related to carrots, and they are similarly sweet but with a distinctive earthy flavour, which blends well with other root vegetables and is also enhanced by spices and garlic.

There is not much to see of the parsnip above ground, except for its inedible leaves. It is the large, swollen root that is the part that is eaten. Some varieties, especially when they are in light, fertile soil, can grow very big – to 45cm/18in or even longer – but for most purposes, smaller roots are more than adequate and usually more flavourful.

HISTORY

Parsnips were developed in Europe from the widespread wild parsnip. It is possible that the Greeks and Romans cultivated them, but there is confusion over whether they were referring to parsnips or carrots in their writings. However, parsnips were certainly being eaten in Europe in the Middle Ages, although they subsequently went into something of a decline (except as cattle food), and it is principally in Britain where they remain popular. Parsnips have always been part of country fare, but they are now regaining a rightful place as vegetables for discerning palates.

VARIETIES

There are more than 30 different varieties of parsnip, which differ only slightly from each other in terms of appearance in the garden and on the plate. Some offer some degree of resistance to canker and some have less hard cores, but your choice will probably be guided by what grows best for you. Because parsnip seed quickly loses its viability, buy fresh seed every year. An opened packet can be kept in a sealed jar or plastic bag in the refrigerator if you are making successional sowings, but the seed should not be kept until the next year.

One of the first parsnips to be developed with disease resistance was 'Avonresister', which has short, rather wide-shouldered roots, which can be grown close together. It can still be found in some catalogues and is a good choice if you are gardening on shallow soil. Another popular variety is 'Tender and True', which also has some resistance to canker; the strongly tapering roots, almost without cores, have an excellent flavour and good

parsnips

Very small parsnips need little or no peeling; just trim the ends and cook according to your recipe. Medium-size and large parsnips should be peeled like potatoes. Larger parsnips also need to have the woody core removed; if it is cut out before cooking, the parsnips will cook more quickly and evenly.

Roast parsnips are best par-boiled for a few minutes before they are added to the roasting dish. Very young parsnips can be roasted whole, but larger ones are best halved or quartered lengthways. Roast in butter or oil for about 40 minutes in an oven preheated to 200°C/400°F/Gas 6.

To boil parsnips, cut them into pieces about 5cm/2in long and boil for 15–20 minutes until tender. If they are boiled briefly like this, they keep their shape, but when added to a casserole or stew they eventually disintegrate. Don't worry if this happens; parsnips need plenty of cooking so that the flavour can blend with the other ingredients.

texture. One of the best modern cultivars, and ideal for small gardens, is 'Gladiator', which is not only canker resistant but is also fast growing. It has smooth, neatly tapering roots and very white flesh. Among the cultivars that can be grown closely together are 'Lancer', 'Arrow' and 'Javelin'.

Among the old varieties is 'The Student', which has been known since 1860. It is a large parsnip, with roots growing to almost 50cm/20in and a mild, sweet flavour. 'Hollow Crown' ('Guernsey', 'Large Sugar') is another traditional parsnip, cultivated since the early 19th

ABOVE Whenever possible, leave parsnips in the ground until after the first frost, which is said to improve the flavour.

century. The smooth, slender, white roots grow to about 36cm/15in long and have well-flavoured white flesh. It is a good choice for deep beds and stores well.

NUTRITION

Parsnips are effective detoxifiers and are believed to fight some cancers. They contain moderate amounts of vitamins A and C, along with some of the B vitamins. They are also a source of calcium, iron, folic acid, potassium and fibre.

Here, parsnips are being blanched with baby onions and carrots in enough water to cover.

Radishes *Raphanus sativus*

The peppery flavour of radishes can almost be felt in the nostrils as you bite into one. Their pungency varies, depending on the variety and also on the soil in which they are grown. Freshly harvested radishes have the most pronounced flavour and a crisp, fresh texture. Both the small red types and the large white radishes are internationally popular.

Radishes are one of the easiest and quickest of all crops to grow. The rapidity with which they appear through the soil makes them suitable for children to grow, because little patience is required, and, indeed, many gardeners' first experience of growing vegetables was with this humble plant. However, the wide range of types and varieties that are available make this a vegetable that is of as much interest to the mature gardener as to the embryonic one.

One of the advantages of the short life-cycle of the radish is that it can be grown among slower-growing crops, thus making the best use of the available ground. Radishes make good markers if they are sown along with a vegetable that is slower to germinate, such as parsnips. Because radish leaves appear quickly, they will indicate the position of the row, so that the parsnip seeds are not accidentally disturbed by hoeing or weeding before they have germinated.

HISTORY

The radish has a long history as far as cultivation is concerned, having been known in Ancient Egypt. Their origins are obscure, but today's radishes are probably derived from native plants found growing in Mediterranean countries. At first, varieties had long, tapering roots, originally black, later white, and these larger-rooted forms are still cultivated in Europe. By the 18th century, however, the more familiar round ones with bright pinkish-red skins and crisp, white flesh began to appear.

VARIETIES

As with many other root vegetables, radishes are often sold in supermarkets and shops simply by their generic name, but many named varieties are available, and it is possible to find radishes that will crop almost all year round and in a range of colours, shapes and sizes. The small, red-skinned varieties, used in salads and garnishes, are the most frequently grown. The early 'Cherry Belle' (globe) has bright red skin and sweet, succulent white flesh that is very slow to go woody. The traditional and reliable 'French Breakfast' (long) has scarlet skin and white

radishes

VARIETIES

Summer
'Cherry Belle' globe
'Crystal Ball' globe
'Flamboyant Sabina' cylindrical
'French Breakfast' cylindrical
'Juliette' globe
'Long White Icicle' tapering
'Prinz Rotin' globe
'Saxa' globe
'Scarlet Globe' globe
'Sparkler 3' globe

Winter
'China Rose'
'Long Black Spanish'
'Mino Early'
'Minowase'
'Round Black Spanish'
'Violet de Gournay'

tips, and the tasty white flesh is crisp and juicy; seed can be planted from early spring right into autumn. 'April Cross' has long, white, cylindrical roots; it shows some resistance to bolting, so is a good choice for an early sowing.

'Long White Icicle' ('Lady's Finger') has tapering white roots, to 12cm/5in long, with an intriguing spicy taste; this is a good choice for summer sowing as it withstands dry conditions well. 'Cherokee' produces large, round, red-skinned roots; the white flesh has a distinctive flavour. 'Duro' (globe) produces large, glossy red roots, almost 10cm/4in across, with gleaming white, juicy flesh, which has a pronounced spicy flavour; it shows good disease resistance and has a long growing period. For

BELOW The elongated French breakfast radish has a mild flavour, which is perfect for salads.

early sowing under glass, try 'Short Top Forcing'.

Increased interest in what are known as heritage vegetables means that some of the older varieties are available through specialist suppliers. If you want winter radishes, look out for 'China Rose' (long), a strongly flavoured radish with white flesh and brilliant red skin. 'Round Black Spanish', which, as the name implies, is a black-skinned variety, grows to almost the size of a turnip; the white flesh has a pungent flavour and the lifted radishes store well in moist sand. 'Long Black Spanish' produces roots to 20cm/8in long; the white flesh is tasty and crisp. A traditional French variety, 'Violet de Gournay', has dark purplish skin. Summer radishes include 'Wood's Frame', which has pink, strongly flavoured, tapering roots to about 8cm/3in long. 'French Golden' has juicy and crunchy roots; if plants are left to run to seed, the pods can be eaten in salads. A fast-growing summer radish, with succulent, crisp flesh, 'Rote Reisen von Aspern' is especially popular in continental Europe, where it is often sold unnamed.

The Chinese radish 'Beauty Heart' ('Mantanghong') has tennis-ball-sized roots with magenta flesh and white or green skins. The crisp, juicy flesh, with a slightly nutty flavour, is ideal in salads.

Mooli or daikon radishes are sometimes sold as oriental radishes. They have long, white roots with smooth skins and a hot, peppery flavour straight from the garden.

PREPARING AND COOKING

Red radishes need only to be washed. They can be sliced or eaten whole by themselves or in salads. You can make a feature of them by slicing a few into a salad of, say, oranges and walnuts, perhaps with a scattering of rocket (arugula) and dressed with a walnut oil vinaigrette. To use moolis in a stir-fry, cut them into slices and add to the dish for the last few minutes of cooking. They add not only flavour but also a wonderfully juicy and crunchy texture.

NUTRITION

Renowned for being a diuretic vegetable, radishes also contain a certain amount of vitamin C. The pungent flavour is produced by glucosinolates.

BELOW The oriental radish, known as a mooli or daikon, resembles a parsnip but has a hot, peppery taste.

Potatoes *Solanum tuberosum*

The potato is one of the most important food crops in the world. The family to which it belongs, Solanaceae, is found worldwide, although the potato itself originates from a fairly restricted area in the Andes. There are many species involved in the botanical development of the potato, which is very complicated, and the history of the potato in cultivation is almost as complicated as its botanical history.

The tubers – that is, the swellings on the roots – are eaten. All other parts, including the leaves and the fruit, are poisonous. If the tubers are exposed to light for any length of time, they turn green, and this discoloured flesh is also poisonous unless it is cooked.

'Epicure'

BELOW 'Estima'

Potatoes are grown from "seed potatoes". These are not actually seeds, but rather potato tubers that have been selected for growing. Once they have been planted, the seed potatoes start to sprout, producing roots and shoots. As the roots grow in the ground, new tubers are formed, and these are harvested when they are large enough to eat.

HISTORY

The potato originates from South America, and was grown as a vegetable in the Andes for thousands of years before the conquering Spanish discovered the Incas eating it in the late 16th century. Taken to Italy, it eventually spread to the rest of Europe. The original cultivars were not particularly hardy, and it took a long time for the potato to catch on in northern Europe and two centuries before it was widespread in Britain. By 1650 potatoes were the staple food of Ireland, and elsewhere in Europe potatoes

VARIETIES

First earlies
'Arran Pilot' white skin
'Epicure' white skin
'Foremost' white skin, waxy yellow flesh
'Maris Bard' white skin, waxy texture
'Pentland Javelin' white skin, waxy flesh
'Ulster Chieftain' white skin, floury texture

Second earlies
'Estima' white skin, waxy yellow flesh, good boiler
'Kondor' red skin, yellow flesh, good boiler
'Marfona' white skin, heavy cropper, good for baking
'Maris Peer' white skin, waxy texture, good boiler
'Wilja' white skin, waxy yellow flesh, good salad potato

Maincrop
'Cara' pink skin, white floury flesh
'Désirée' pinkish red skin, waxy yellow flesh, good for baking and for fries
'King Edward' pink and white skin, creamy floury texture, good for baking and roasting
'Maris Piper' white skin, floury texture, heavy cropper, good for baking
'Pentland Dell' white skin, floury texture, heavy cropper, good for baking and roasting
'Pink Fir Apple' pink skin, yellow waxy flesh, wonderful salad potato
'Ratte' white skin, yellow waxy flesh, excellent salad potato
'Romano' red skin, firm white flesh, good boiler

began to replace wheat as the most important crop, both for people and for livestock.

The first mention of potatoes in the USA dates from 1719 in Londonderry, New Hampshire. They arrived not from the south, but with Irish settlers who brought their potatoes with them.

The current popularity of potatoes is probably thanks to a Frenchman called Antoine-Auguste Parmentier. A military pharmacist of the latter part of the 18th century, Parmentier recognized the virtues of the potato, both for its versatility and as an important food for the poor, and set out to improve its image. He persuaded Louis XVI to let him ostentatiously grow potatoes on royal land around the palace in Versailles to impress the fashion-conscious Parisians. He also produced a court dinner in which each course contained potatoes. Gradually, eating potatoes became chic, first among people in the French court and then in French society. Today, if you see Parmentier in a recipe or on a menu, it means "with potato".

'Wilja'

'Marfona'

VARIETIES

Because potatoes are such an important food crop, hundreds of named varieties have been developed over the years, many suited to particular growing conditions and climates and others to cropping at different times of year. Disease-resistant cultivars have also been hybridized, notably to resist blight, which can wipe out an entire crop and led to famine in Ireland in the 19th century. Most potatoes are classified as earlies or maincrop, which are sometimes further subdivided as first earlies and so on. Another important difference between varieties is the use to which they are put. Some potatoes are better for boiling or mashing, some for roasting or frying, and some for salads. One of the most significant characteristics for the gardener, however, is the difference in flavour among varieties, and many gardeners have their own particular favourites, which they grow year after year.

This is a pity, because the number of varieties is increasing steadily, and new and reintroduced heritage cultivars offer gardeners the most wonderful opportunities to experiment with heavy-cropping and well-flavoured potatoes.

Good, reliable earlies include 'Epicure', 'Foremost', 'Accent' and 'Arran Pilot', which are well-flavoured, high-yielding varieties. 'Home Guard' is a rather floury early, while the recently introduced

'Lady Christi' is a good cropper. 'Duke of York' and 'Red Duke of York' are well flavoured but rather susceptible to blight, but if they are not all harvested, the tubers can be left in the ground to grow on. In a small garden try the fast-growing 'Swift', which has less topgrowth than many potatoes and so takes up less space and can even be grown under a cloche. Another recommendable fast-growing early for a small plot is 'Rocket'.

One of the best-known second earlies is 'Estima', a high-yielding potato with good blight resistance. 'Wilja' and 'Nadine' are excellent, all-purpose, reliable potatoes, which cook well. Other good second earlies include 'Charlotte', the yellow-skinned 'Nicola' and

LEFT 'Désirée'

BELOW 'King Edward'

ROASTING

Peel the potatoes and cut them into even-size pieces. Blanch them in boiling water for 2–5 minutes, drain, then shake in the pan or fork over the surfaces to roughen them up.

Pour a shallow layer of your chosen fat into a good heavy roasting pan and place it in the oven, heating it to a temperature of 220°C/425°F/Gas 7. Add the dry, forked potatoes and toss immediately in the hot fat.

Return to the top shelf of the oven and roast for up to one hour, until tender. Once or twice during cooking, remove the roasting pan from the oven and, using a spatula, turn the potatoes over to evenly coat them in fat.

ABOVE 'Maris Piper'

ABOVE 'Pentland Dell'

ABOVE 'Pink Fir Apple'

the red-skinned 'Roseval', which are waxy potatoes that are ideal for using in salads.

One of the best-known maincrop potatoes is the popular 'King Edward', and although it does not always crop as well as some of the more recent introductions the tubers are always good quality. The high-yielding, red-skinned 'Désirée' is noted for its good cooking qualities, while 'Maris Piper' is good for frying or chips. The vigorous 'Cara', with a red-blotched skin like 'King Edward', shows good resistance to both blight and drought. The traditional 'Pink Fir Apple', a late-maturing potato for lifting in autumn, has unusual, long, knobbly, pinkish tubers; this is an especially good salad potato, with a good flavour and waxy texture, and the tubers keep well in winter. Blight-resistant maincrop varieties include 'Romano' and 'Santée', which is a popular choice among organic gardeners.

Among the traditional varieties is 'Belle de Fontenay', which produces smooth, yellow tubers

with an excellent flavour and waxy texture, which are ideal for salads; it is not resistant to blight. 'Witch Hill' ('Snowdrop') has floury, smooth, white tubers and is resistant to potato wart disease. The unusual 'Edzell Blue', a traditional Scottish variety, has tubers with a blue-purple skin and white flesh; it is grown as an early maincrop. 'Vitelotte Noire' ('La Nigresse'), which was first grown in France, not only has blue skin but also blue flesh, and it retains the colour after cooking. It is a good potato for salads.

NUTRITION

Potatoes are an important source of carbohydrate. Once thought to be fattening, we now know that, on the contrary, potatoes can be an excellent part of a calorie-controlled diet – provided, of course, that they are not fried in oil or mashed with too much butter. Potatoes are also an excellent source of vitamin C, and during the winter months potatoes are often

the main source of this vitamin. They also contain potassium, iron and vitamins B3 and B6.

SWEET POTATOES

Sweet potatoes (*Ipomeoea batatas*) are native to tropical America, but today they are grown all over the tropical world. They are an important staple food in the Caribbean and southern United States, and many famous recipes feature these vegetables. Candied sweet potatoes, for instance, are traditionally served with ham or turkey at Thanksgiving all over the USA, while the islands of the West Indies abound with sweet potato dishes, from the simple baked potato to Caribbean pudding, a typically sweet and spicy dish with sweet potatoes, coconut, limes and cinnamon.

Salsify and scorzonera
Tragopogon porrifolius and *Scorzonera hispanica*

Although salsify and scorzonera are different plants, they are closely related, not only botanically but also in the manner in which they are grown and used. Scorzonera is, in fact, sometimes confusingly known as black salsify. Neither is in the mainstream of vegetables, which is surprising because both are delicious. Salsify is also known as vegetable oyster or oyster plant, perhaps because of its nutty taste or its glossy appearance. The roots are, however, not among the easiest to prepare – they are relatively narrow with plenty of smaller roots, which makes peeling difficult. In addition, they discolour very quickly once they have been peeled. In the kitchen, despite the fine taste, they are not very versatile since they are

ABOVE The roots of the biennial salsify are long and creamy brown, rather similar to parsnips.

usually used as vegetables in their own right rather than as part of other dishes.

VARIETIES

Salsify
Most are listed simply as salsify or vegetable oyster.
'Mammoth'
'Sandwich Island'

Scorzonera
Most are listed simply as scorzonera.
'Duplex'
'Lange Jan'
'Maxima'
'Russian Giant'

Both vegetables have long, narrow taproots, which are covered in thinner side roots. Salsify has a yellowish skin, rather like that of a parsnip, and scorzonera has a dark brown or black skin. They are grown mainly for the roots, but the young shoots and flowerbuds of both can also be eaten in salads. Salsify is also grown as an ornamental plant for its attractive purple flowers, although the leaves can be rather untidy. The flowers produce copious amounts of seed, which soon drifts away and germinates. Scorzonera has inconspicuous yellow flowers.

HISTORY
Salsify originated from the countries around the Mediterranean, although garden escapees have naturalized over a large part of Europe and North America. Scorzonera is not quite as rampant and is still restricted to Europe, from the warm

salsify

Salsify and scorzonera are difficult to clean and peel. Either scrub the root under cold running water and then peel after cooking, or peel with a sharp stainless steel knife. Because the flesh discolours quickly, place the trimmed pieces into acidulated water (water to which a little lemon juice has been added).

To cook, cut into short lengths and simmer for 20–30 minutes until tender. Drain well and sauté in butter, or serve with lemon juice, melted butter or chopped parsley. Alternatively, they can be puréed for soups or mashed. Cooked and cooled salsify and scorzonera can be served in a mustard or garlic vinaigrette with a simple salad.

Mediterranean countries to the Arctic wastes. As with most vegetables, their history is rather uncertain, but salsify is thought to have been first cultivated in Italy in the 16th century, while scorzonera was grown in Spain and Italy even earlier.

Both roots are classified as herbs and, like many wild plants and herbs, their history is bound up with their use in medicines. The roots, together with their leaves and flowers, were used for the treatment of heartburn, loss of appetite and various liver diseases.

VARIETIES

Both salsify and scorzonera are usually available only as unnamed forms, although there are a few named cultivars, and as interest in traditional varieties increases more are likely to offered by specialist suppliers. One of the most often

ABOVE The perennial scorzonera has long roots with black skin. It can be left in the ground to grow on if the roots are not large enough to eat.

found named varieties of salsify is 'Sandwich Island', which has been grown in Europe since the close of the 19th century. It produces roots that look rather like slender parsnips. They are creamy white and grow to about 25cm/10in long. If possible, leave the roots in the ground until after the first frosts, which is said to improve the flavour. 'Giant', 'Mammoth White' and 'Mammoth Sandwich Island' are similar but larger.

Among the named varieties of scorzonera is 'Russian Giant' ('Géante Noire de Russe'), which has the tapering, black-skinned, white roots typical of the plant. The roots of this variety, which are ideal for inclusion in stews and soups,

grow to 45cm/18in in the right conditions, and they can be left in the ground for a year to develop and thicken. It is thought that scorzonera helps to repel carrot root fly when it is grown among carrots.

NUTRITION

The sweet flesh of scorzonera contains the carbohydrate inulin, which is composed of fructose, making it suitable for diabetics.

planning and
preparation

Most root crops will produce better yields if they are grown in a vegetable plot, rather than being scattered around the garden. This is largely a matter of practicality, because root crops, by their nature, will be lifted when they reach maturity, and few gardeners will want large gaps in their decorative borders through the growing season. Even a small area dedicated to root vegetables will provide tasty crops over a long period from summer to winter, and with a little forward planning and careful selection of cultivars, this can be one of the most rewarding and productive parts of the garden.

Types of soil

Root vegetables can be grown on almost any type of ground, but because most are greedy feeders, it is important to make sure that the soil is not only well-drained and moisture-retentive but also fertile. Maintaining the soil in good condition will quickly become a routine once you have determined the type of soil that you have in your garden. You can buy kits that show both the pH and the level of nutrients in garden soil, so that you can provide the perfect conditions for your chosen crops.

CLAY SOIL

Although clay soil is often fertile, it can be difficult and heavy to work, and the particles cling together, making the soil sticky. Clay soil compacts easily, forming solid

TESTING THE SOIL

Check soil samples 5–8cm/2–3in below the surface. Take a number of samples, and test each one separately. Potatoes grow best in a very rich soil that is more acid than neutral, around a pH of 5–6.

lumps that roots find hard to penetrate and making it difficult to dig. Try not to walk on clay soil when it is wet, which will compact the soil even more. In addition, clay soil is slow to drain in wet weather, but, once it has drained, it can set like concrete. It can also be cold and slow to warm up in spring, making it unsuitable for early crops. On the other hand, clay soil is slow to cool down in autumn, and it can be easily improved by the addition of well-rotted compost or manure and made easier to handle by the incorporation of grit.

SANDY SOIL

Soils made up of sand and silts are composed of individual grains that allow water to pass through them quickly, and this speedy passage of water through the soil tends to leach (wash) out nutrients. Sandy soils are often rather poor and do not retain moisture well. However, they can be quick to warm up in spring, making them ideal for early crops. Silty soil contains particles that are more clay-like in texture than those found in sandy soils, and they hold more moisture and nutrients. Both types of soil are easy to improve and are not difficult to work. Sand does not compact as clay does, although it is still not good practice to walk on beds, but silty soil is susceptible to the impact of feet. Adding plenty of well-rotted organic material will make both types more moisture-retentive.

pH VALUES

1.0	extremely acid
4.0	maximum acidity tolerated by most plants
5.5	maximum acidity for reasonable vegetables
6.0	maximum acidity for most fruit and vegetables
6.5	optimum for the best fruit and vegetables
7.0	neutral, maximum alkalinity for good fruit and vegetables
7.5	maximum alkalinity for reasonable vegetables
8.0	maximum tolerated by most plants
14.0	extremely alkaline

LOAM

This type of soil is a combination of clay and sandy soils, with the best characteristics of both. It tends to be both free-draining and also moisture-retentive, and although this may seem to be a contradiction in terms, it means that the soil is sufficiently free-draining to allow excess water to drain away easily, ensuring that air is available to the roots, but enough moisture is retained for plants to be able to take up nutrients from the soil. Loamy soil is the ideal for which gardeners strive. It is easy to work at almost any time of the year and warms up well in spring.

ACID AND ALKALINE SOILS

Soils are also sometimes classified by their acidity or alkalinity. Those that are based on peat (peat moss) are acid; those that include chalk or limestone are alkaline. A scale of pH levels is used to indicate the degree of acidity and alkalinity. Neutral soil has a pH of 7; a pH lower than that indicates acidity, while a pH above 7 indicates an alkaline soil. Most root vegetables will do best in slightly acid to neutral soil, although potatoes prefer more acid conditions. Use one of the simple testing kits to check the soil in your garden. Take samples from several places about 8cm/3in down and follow the manufacturer's instructions.

AMENDING SOIL PH

If you find that your soil has a pH below 5.5, which indicates acid conditions, you can adjust the pH upwards by adding lime to the soil. Mushroom compost, which is rich in lime, can be used instead.

IMPROVING SOIL FERTILITY

The fertility of the soil is much improved by the addition of organic material, but a quick boost can also be achieved by adding an organic fertilizer, spreading it over the surface and then raking it in.

It is more difficult to reduce the pH levels of alkaline soils, and the traditional method of digging in peat is now environmentally unacceptable. In any case, most soils tend to be slightly acid because calcium is continually leached out by rainfall. If the pH of the soil in your garden is too extreme for cultivating vegetables, consider using raised beds, which you can fill with topsoil bought in from elsewhere.

IMPROVING SOIL QUALITY

The most important task in the garden is to improve and maintain the quality of the soil. Good-quality soil is the aim of any gardener who wants to grow a range of root vegetables, and to ignore the quality of the soil will lead to poor yields and plants that are susceptible to pests and diseases. The key to improving the soil in your garden is well-rotted organic material. To the gardener, this term covers any vegetable matter that has been broken down into an odourless, fibrous compost. It includes such things as rotted garden waste, vegetable waste from the kitchen, farmyard manure and other plant waste material.

It is important that such material is well rotted. If it is still in the process of rotting down when it is applied to the soil, it will extract nitrogen from the soil as it continues to break down. This is, of course, the opposite of what the gardener wants – the aim is to add nitrogen to the soil. A good indicator that the material has broken down is

TESTING THE SOIL FOR NUTRIENTS

Collect the soil sample 5–8cm/ 2–3in below the surface. Take a number of samples, but test each one separately. With the kit shown, mix one part of soil with five parts of water. Shake well in a jar, then allow the water to settle. Draw off some of the settled liquid from the top few centimetres (about an inch) for your test. Carefully transfer the solution to the test chamber in the plastic container, using the pipette. Select a colour-coded capsule (one for each different nutrient). Put the powder in the chamber, replace the cap and shake well. After a few minutes, compare the colour of the liquid with the shade panel of the container.

that it is odourless. Even horse manure is free from odour once it has rotted down. Some bought-in manure contains undesirable chemicals, but these will be removed if the material is stacked and allowed to weather. Bark and other shredded woody materials may contain resins, for example, while animal and bird manures may contain ammonia from urea. These chemicals will evaporate or be converted during weathering.

Soil conditioners

A wide range of organic soil conditioners is available to the gardener. Some are free – if you do not count the time taken in working and carting them. Others are relatively cheap, and some, usually those bought by the bag, can be quite expensive.

FARMYARD MANURE

A traditional material and still much used by many country gardeners, farmyard manure has the advantage of adding bulk to the soil as well as supplying valuable nutrients. The manure can come from any form of livestock, although the most commonly available is horse manure. It can be obtained from most stables, and many are so glad to get rid of it that they will supply it free if you fetch it yourself. There are often stables situated around the edge of towns, so manure is usually available to town gardeners as well as to those in the country. However, not everyone has a stable nearby or enough space to store large quantities of material, and many gardeners will therefore need to buy it as required.

Some gardeners do not like the manure when it is mixed with wood shavings rather than with straw, but it is worth bearing in mind that the former is often less likely to contain weed seeds, and as long as it is stacked and allowed to rot down thoroughly it is excellent both for adding to the soil and for use as a top-dressing.

All manures should be stacked for a period of at least six months before they are used. When the manure is ready to use, it will have lost its dungy smell.

GARDEN COMPOST

All gardeners should make an effort to recycle as much of their garden and kitchen vegetable waste as possible. In essence, this is simply following nature's pattern, where leaves and stems are formed in the

spring and die back in the autumn, falling to the ground and eventually rotting and returning to the plants as nutrients. In the garden some things are removed from the cycle, notably vegetables and fruit, but as much as possible should be returned to the earth.

Compost is not difficult to make. If you have the space, use several bins, so that there is always one ready for use while you fill another.

Unless seeding or perennial weeds or diseased plants have been used, compost should be safe to use as a soil conditioner and as a mulch. From the kitchen, it is best to avoid meat, fats and cooked foods, which attract vermin.

LEAF MOULD

This is another natural soil conditioner. It is easy to make and should not cost anything. Only use leaf mould made by yourself; never go down to the local woods and help yourself because this will disturb the wood's own cycle and will impoverish the soil there.

Four stakes knocked into the ground with a piece of wire netting stretched around them will make

GREEN MANURE

Broad (fava) beans: nitrogen fixing
Italian ryegrass: quick growing
Lupins: nitrogen fixing
Mustard: quick growing
Phacelia: quick growing
Red clover: nitrogen fixing
Winter tare: nitrogen fixing

ORGANIC MATERIALS

Well-rotted farmyard manure

Well-rotted garden compost

the perfect container for making leaf mould. Simply add the leaves as they fall from deciduous trees. It will take a couple of years for them to break down and what was a huge heap will have shrunk to a small layer by the time the process is complete.

Add leaf mould to the soil or use it as a top-dressing. It is usually acid and can be used to reduce the pH of alkaline soil. Conifer needles, which should be stored separately, produce a leaf mould that is particularly acid.

PEAT (PEAT MOSS)

This is expensive and does little for the soil because it breaks down too quickly and has little nutritive content. However, the reasons for not using it have nothing to do with its nutritional content. Peat (peat moss) is taken from bogs, rare and fragile ecosystems that are rapidly being depleted. Gardeners do not need to use peat and should always look for environmentally responsible alternatives.

SPENT MUSHROOM COMPOST

Often available locally from mushroom farms, the spent compost is relatively cheap, especially if it is purchased in bulk. It is mainly used as a top-dressing in the ornamental part of the garden, but it is still useful in the vegetable garden if it is allowed to rot down. You should allow for the fact that it contains lime, and so will increase the alkalinity of the soil, making it unsuitable for potatoes.

VEGETABLE INDUSTRIAL WASTE

Several industries produce organic waste material that can be useful in the garden. Spent hop waste from the brewing industry is a favourite among those who can obtain it. Cocoa shells are now imported, although these are better used as a mulch than as a soil conditioner. They are comparatively high in nitrogen. Several other products are locally available. Allow them to rot well before using.

ABOVE Green manure can be grown as a separate crop or it can be grown between existing crops. It can fix nitrogen in the soil and acts as a good ground cover.

GREEN MANURE

Some crops can be grown to be dug back into the ground to improve the soil condition and add nutrients. They are useful on light soils that are vacant for any length of time. Green manures can be sown in early autumn and dug in spring.

WORKING IN ORGANIC MATTER

1 Soil that has been dug in the autumn can have more organic matter worked into the top layer in the spring.

2 Lightly work the organic material into the top layer of soil with a fork. There is no need for full-scale digging.

Compost

This is a valuable material for any garden, but it is especially useful in the vegetable garden. It is free, apart from any capital required in installing compost bins – since these should last for many years, the overall cost should be negligible. A little effort is required, but this is a small price to pay for the resulting gold dust.

THE PRINCIPLE

In making compost, gardeners emulate the natural process in which a plant takes nutrients from the soil, dies and then rots, so the nutrients return to the ground. In the garden, waste plant material is collected, piled in a heap and allowed to rot down before being returned to the soil as crumbly, sweet-smelling, fibrous material.

Because it is kept in a heap, the rotting material generates heat, which encourages it to break down more quickly. The heat also helps to kill pests and diseases, as well as

any weed seed in the compost. The balance of air and moisture is important; if the heap is too wet it will go slimy, but if it is too dry it will not decompose. The best balance is achieved by having some ventilation, but protecting the compost from rain, and by using a good mixture of materials.

The process should take up to about three months, but many old-fashioned gardeners like to retain the heap for much longer than that, growing marrows and courgettes (zucchini) on it before they break it up for use in the garden.

THE COMPOST BIN

Gardeners always seem to generate more garden waste than they ever thought possible and never to have enough compost space, so when planning your bins, make sure you have enough. The ideal aim is to have three: one to hold new waste, one that is in the process of breaking down, and a third that is ready for use.

Bins are traditionally made from wood (often scrap wood), and because these can be hand-made to fit your space and the amount of material available, this is still the best

LEFT Good compost is dark brown, crumbly and has a sweet, earthy smell, not a rotting one.

ABOVE A range of organic materials can be used, but avoid cooked kitchen waste or any weeds that have seed in them. Clockwise from top left: kitchen waste, weeds, shreddings and grass clippings.

option. Sheet materials, such as corrugated iron, can also be used. Most ready-made bins are made of plastic, and although these work perfectly well, they may be a bit on the small side in a busy garden.

You can make compost successfully in a bin the size of a dustbin (trash can), but if you have room, one holding a cubic metre/35 cubic feet, or even bigger, will be much more efficient.

The simplest bin can be made by nailing together four wooden pallets to form a box. If the front is made so that the slats are slotted in to form the wall, they can be removed as the bin is emptied, making the job of removing the compost easier.

MATERIALS

Most garden plant waste can be used for composting, but do not include perennial weeds. Weed seeds will be killed if the compost heats up really well, but it is safest not to include them. You could have a separate bin for anything that contains seeds, and use the resulting compost only for permanent plantings such as trees – if the compost never comes to the surface, seeds will not germinate. Woody material, such as hedge clippings, can be used, but shred it first. Kitchen vegetable waste, such as peelings and cores, can be used, but avoid cooked vegetables and do not include meat, which will attract rats and other vermin.

TECHNIQUE

Placing a few branches or twiggy material in the bottom of the bin will help to keep the contents aerated. Put in the material as it becomes available, but avoid building up deep layers of any one material, especially grass cuttings. Mix them with other materials.

To help keep the heap warm, cover it with an old carpet or sheet of plastic. This also prevents excess water from chilling the contents and swamping the air spaces. The lid should be kept on until the compost is needed.

Every so often, add a layer of farmyard manure if you can get it, because it will provide extra nitrogen to speed things up. Failing this, you can buy special compost accelerators. It is not essential to add manure or an accelerator, however – it just means waiting a couple of months longer.

Air is important, and this usually percolates through the side of the bin, so leave a few gaps between the timbers. If you use old pallets, these are usually crudely made, with plenty of gaps. The colder material around the edges takes longer to break down, so turn the compost around every so often. This also loosens the pile and allows air to circulate.

MAKING COMPOST

1 To make garden compost, place a layer of "browns" – straw, dry leaves and chipped wood are ideal – into the bin, to a depth of about 15cm/6in.

2 Begin a layer of "greens" – any green plant material, except perennial or seeding weeds. Fibrous or woody stems should be cut up small or shredded.

3 Add greens until you have a layer 15cm/6in thick. Mix lawn clippings with other green waste to avoid the layer becoming slimy and airless.

4 Kitchen refuse, including fruit and vegetable waste and eggshells, can be added, but not cooked or fatty foods. Cover the heap.

5 Turn the heap occasionally. The speed of composting will vary, but when ready, the compost should be brown, crumbly and sweet-smelling.

Fertilizers

In nature, when plants die down they return the nutrients they have taken from the soil. In the garden, the vegetables are removed and the chain is broken. Compost and other organic materials help to redress the balance, but they may not be able to do the job properly and then fertilizers are needed, applied at regular intervals.

WHAT PLANTS REQUIRE

The main foods required by plants are nitrogen (N), phosphorus (P) and potassium (K), with smaller quantities of magnesium (Mg), calcium (Ca) and sulphur (S). They also require small amounts of trace elements, including iron (Fe) and manganese (Mn). Each of the main nutrients tends to be used by the plant for one specific function.

Nitrogen is used for promoting the rapid growth of the green parts of the plant. Phosphorus, usually in the form of phosphates, is used to create good root growth as well as helping with the ripening of fruits, while potassium, in the form of potash, is used to promote flowering and formation of good fruit.

ORGANIC FERTILIZERS

Concentrated fertilizers are of two types: organic and inorganic. Organic fertilizers consist solely of naturally occurring materials and contain different proportions of nutrients. So bonemeal (ground-up bones), which is strong in phosphates and nitrogen, promotes growth, especially root growth. Bonemeal also has the advantage that it breaks down slowly and gradually, releasing the fertilizer over a long period. (Wear gloves when you apply bonemeal.)

Other organic fertilizers include fish, blood and bone (high in nitrogen and phosphates); hoof and horn (nitrogen); and seaweed meal (nitrogen and potash). Because they are derived from natural products without any modification, they are used by organic growers.

INORGANIC FERTILIZERS

These fertilizers have been made artificially, although they are frequently derived from natural rocks and minerals and the process may just involve crushing. They are concentrated and are usually soluble in water, which means that they are instantly available for the plant. They do, however, tend to wash out of the soil quickly and need to be replaced.

Some inorganic formulations are general fertilizers, and might contain equal proportions of nitrogen, phosphorus and potassium, for example. Others are much more specific. Superphosphate, for example, is entirely used for supplying phosphorus, while potassium sulphate is added to the soil if potassium is required.

SLOW-RELEASE FERTILIZERS

A modern trend is to coat the fertilizers so that they are released slowly into the soil. These are expensive in the short term, but because they do not leach away and do not need to be replaced as frequently, they can be considered more economic in the longer term.

They are particularly useful for container planting, where constant watering is necessary, which dissolves and washes away normal fertilizer, but are less often used in the open garden.

ORGANIC FERTILIZERS

blood   bonemeal

seaweed   fish/blood/bone

INORGANIC FERTILIZERS

Growmore (not available in USA)   sulphate of ammonia

potash   superphosphate

Digging the soil

If you are thinking about growing root vegetables for the first time, you should consider double digging the area. This will enable you to remove any large stones and the roots of any perennial weeds, which will be difficult to remove once crops are growing. The process will also aerate and break up any compacted soil, thereby improving the drainage, and give you an opportunity to dig in plenty of well-rotted manure where the roots can easily get to it. Double digging involves removing two spade depths of soil. Because it is important that the subsoil is kept separate from the topsoil, place two plastic sheets on the ground next to the plot so that you can pile the topsoil and subsoil from each trench on a different sheet before you replace them in the next trench.

The value of digging every year has been questioned, however. Provided the soil was well cultivated in the first instance, further digging may do more harm than good to the structure, and many gardeners prefer not to do it.

DOUBLE DIGGING

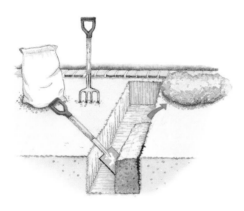

1 Dig a wide trench, placing the soil to one side to be used later when filling in the final trench.

2 Break up the soil at the bottom of the trench, adding manure to the soil as you proceed.

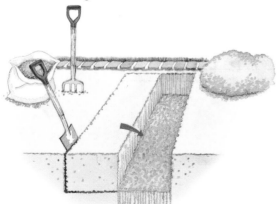

3 Dig the next trench, turning the soil over on top of the broken soil in the first trench.

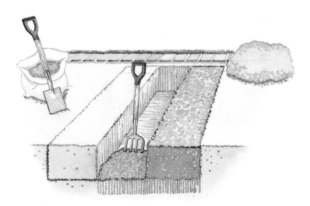

4 Continue down the plot, ensuring that subsoil from the lower trench is not mixed with topsoil from the upper.

Garden tools

Looking in the average garden centre, you would imagine that you need a tremendous battery of tools and equipment before you could ever consider gardening, but in fact you can start (and continue) gardening with relatively few.

Tools are personal things, so one gardener may always use a spade for digging, no matter how soft the ground, whereas another would always use a fork as long as the ground was not too heavy. The type of hoe for a particular job is another subject on which gardeners hold widely different opinions.

TYPES OF TOOLS

The main types of tools that are useful for cultivating most root vegetables are a fork, spade, one or more hoes, and a rake.

A fork is used for general cultivation, lifting vegetables, aerating the soil, moving bulky organic material and incorporating it into the soil. A spade is essential for digging, general cultivation and deep weed control.

There are several different types of hoe: cultivator; draw or swan-neck; and push, plate or Dutch.

A cultivator is a form of three-pronged hoe that is very good for weeding between rows of vegetables. The tool is drawn between the rows to loosen the earth and with it any seedlings that have just germinated. As their roots are loose in the soil they cannot pick up moisture, so they die.

A draw hoe or swan-neck hoe is pulled towards the gardener in a series of chopping movements. This removes weeds by scraping them off as the hoe is drawn back. In contrast, a push, plate or Dutch hoe is pushed forwards, slicing off the weeds. Hoes are best used in dry weather because they do not open the soil too much, which causes evaporation. In wet weather, however, the cultivator can be useful because it opens the soil and allows the water to drain through.

A rake is essential for breaking up and levelling soil when a vegetable plot is being prepared.

BUYING TOOLS

Most jobs can be done with a small basic kit of tools. When you are buying, always choose the best you can afford. Many cheaper tools are

made of pressed steel, which soon becomes blunt, will often bend and may even break. Stainless steel is undoubtedly the best but tends to be expensive. Ordinary steel implements can be almost as good, especially if you keep them clean. Trowels and hand forks especially are often made of aluminium, but they wear down and blunt quickly and are not good value for money.

SECOND-HAND

A good way to get a collection of tools is to buy them second-hand, which will be much cheaper than buying new ones. Usually, too, they will be made of better steel than modern ones and still retain a keen edge, even after many years' use.

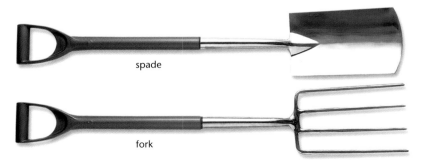

spade

fork

In the past gardening tools were made with a greater variation in design and size. If you go to buy a modern spade, for example, you will probably find that the sizes are all the same – designed for the "average" gardener. Old tools come in all shapes and sizes, and if you find modern tools uncomfortable to use you are more likely to find an old one that suits you.

Not all old tools are good by any means, of course, but by keeping an eye out and buying only good quality ones you will end up with tools that will see you through your gardening career. Car boot sales (garage sales) and rural junk shops (second-hand stores) are the places to look out for them. Avoid antique shops, where such tools are sold at inflated prices to be hung on the wall as decorations rather than used for gardening.

CARE AND MAINTENANCE

If you look after your tools they will always be in good working condition and will last a lifetime. Scrape off mud and vegetation as soon as you have used the tools. Once they are clean, run an oily rag lightly over the metal parts. The thin film of oil will stop the metal from corroding. As well as helping

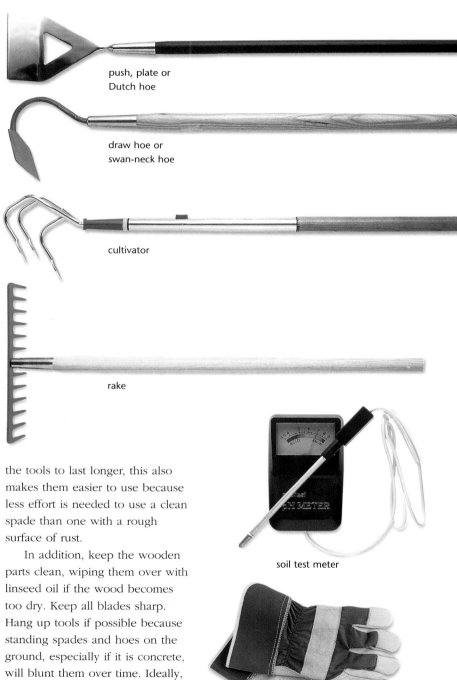

push, plate or
Dutch hoe

draw hoe or
swan-neck hoe

cultivator

rake

soil test meter

gloves

the tools to last longer, this also makes them easier to use because less effort is needed to use a clean spade than one with a rough surface of rust.

In addition, keep the wooden parts clean, wiping them over with linseed oil if the wood becomes too dry. Keep all blades sharp. Hang up tools if possible because standing spades and hoes on the ground, especially if it is concrete, will blunt them over time. Ideally, keep your tools in a shed or garage, where they can be kept locked away. Keep all tools safely away from children.

trowel

hand fork

Pests and diseases

The list of potential pests and diseases that can affect root vegetables can so alarm gardeners that they decide not to try growing them at all. This is a shame, because as long as the vegetable plot is kept well weeded and well fertilized, the healthy, vigorous plants will be able to fend off most problems. For some gardeners one of the most difficult aspects of controlling problems is to be completely ruthless about digging up and throwing away or burning crops that are diseased. It is far better to have a gap in the garden for a few months than to allow a disease or pest to become endemic.

CABBAGE ROOT FLY

All members of the brassica family are susceptible to this serious pest. The larvae live in the soil, feeding on the roots of young plants. If they are not controlled they can, at worst, completely destroy the plant or, at best, stunt the plants so that they do not crop well. As always, prevention is better than cure, and placing a floating mulch of horticultural fleece over the bed or protecting it with fine-mesh netting supported on sticks will stop the insects laying eggs in the ground. (This will also protect plants from other insect pests, including flea beetles.) If you have only a few plants, placing a collar, about 15cm/6in square, of roofing felt or a similar material around the stem of each transplanted seedling will prevent the adults laying eggs in the surrounding soil.

CARROT FLY

This is an important pest not only for carrots, but also for parsnips. As with cabbage root fly, the damage is done by the soil-dwelling larvae, which eat the roots. The flies are attracted to the garden by the smell of damaged carrots or crushed carrot foliage, and this is why it is so important to thin seedlings on dull evenings, when the flies are less active. Erecting a fine-mesh fence, about 45cm/18in high, around the vegetable plot will help to deter the low-flying insects from reaching your crops.

FLEA BEETLE

The seedlings of brassicas are susceptible to damage from flea beetles, which are tiny insects that eat numerous small holes in the leaves. Severe infestations are best tackled by dusting the young plants with derris. Strongly growing plants are rarely badly affected. To deter this pest, clear all debris away at the end of the season so that the beetles cannot overwinter.

SLUGS AND SNAILS

The circular holes in many root crops and the large cavities in potatoes are usually caused by slugs, and digging up roots and tubers promptly is important if you have a lot of slugs in your garden. Both slugs and snails will also eat the above-ground parts of plants. Pellets (metaldehyde or methiocarb) or metaldehyde spray will kill them, but birds can then be poisoned by eating the dead slugs. It is far better to control

LEFT Biological controls are mainly used in greenhouses, but others are now becoming available for the open garden. The control insects are released, here from a sachet, in order to attack the pests.

ABOVE Carrot fly will eat holes in the roots of carrots and parsnips.

soil-dwelling slugs by using a biological control, nematodes, which can be watered into the soil in late summer. At night go out and collect all the slugs and snails you can see, putting them in a bucket of water so that you can dispose of them. Dishes of beer sunk in the ground and upturned grapefruit skins can also be used to attract slugs, and some gardeners like to leave surplus seedlings near the vegetable plot so that slugs and snails will be attracted to the waste rather than to the crops themselves.

WIREWORM

Narrow but extensive tunnels are made in roots and tubers by the larvae of click beetles, which are a problem in grassed areas that have recently been brought into cultivation. The problem usually disappears once ground has been cultivated for four or five years, during which time the larvae will have been exposed to birds. In the meantime, lift tubers as soon as

they are ready. Water in pirimiphos-methyl or treat the soil at the start of the growing season with lindane or chlorpyrifos and diazinon.

BLIGHT

This is the most serious disease of potatoes, and it spreads quickly in warm, humid weather. The fungus infects leaves, stems and tubers. Yellow-brown patches appear on the leaves, and in dry weather they become dry and brown. In wet weather the leaves, then the stems, turn black and rot, and a white fungal growth can be seen under the leaves. Infected tubers have dark, sunken patches on the skin, and a red-brown discoloration may spread to the flesh. Once a plant is infected, the only cure is to cut off all the topgrowth and throw it away (don't compost it) or burn it. Leave the tubers in the ground for two or three weeks, and dig them up on a dry day. Choosing resistant cultivars, deep planting and careful earthing (hilling) up will help to prevent the spores entering the ground.

CANKER

Different types of canker can attack specific crops, and some cultivars have been developed to be resistant to the relevant form of the disease. The parsnip 'Avonresister', for example, has been bred for resistance to parsnip canker. It can be a problem in soils that lack lime, but it is more likely to infect crops that have already been damaged by careless hoeing to remove weeds or by an insect pest, such as carrot fly.

CLUB ROOT

This is one of the most serious problems affecting all members of the brassica family, both vegetable and ornamental. It badly distorts the roots and topgrowth, and it is potentially so serious because it persists in the ground for many, many years. It can be worse on very acid soil, and applications of lime to raise the pH to 6.5–7.5 may help to prevent it. Infected plants should be immediately dug up and thrown away or burned.

BELOW Slugs and snails have few friends among gardeners. They make holes in just about any part of a plant, often leaving it useless or even dead.

Growing root vegetables organically

As increasing numbers of people become concerned about the levels of chemical insecticides, fertilizers and fungicides used to mass-produce attractive, uniform-looking vegetables at the lowest possible cost, the attractions of growing just a few vegetables on organic principles become ever greater. This is especially the case with root vegetables, which are known to absorb and retain high levels of chemicals from the soil.

MAKING THE CHANGE

Many gardeners are deterred from abandoning all chemical aids because there can be no doubt that, at first, a garden run on organic-only lines does see a slight increase in the level of pests and diseases, especially diseases transmitted by insect pests. This is a temporary problem, however, and as soon as a good balance is established, the incidence of both pests and diseases will begin to fall. As the number of beneficial insects in a garden increases, insect pests will be greatly reduced. Natural predators, ranging from blue tits and hedgehogs to hoverflies and lacewings, will thrive in an organic garden, but it will take some time for populations to become established and to build up to levels where they can be effective in controlling the levels of insect pests.

FEEDING THE SOIL

Rather than adding chemical fertilizers to the soil, organic gardeners prefer to add organic matter, such as well-rotted manure or garden compost, spent

ABOVE Green manure helps to improve both the structure and fertility of the soil. Sow it when the ground is not being used for anything else and then dig it in before it flowers and sets seed.

mushroom compost and seaweed, which have the added advantage of improving the texture of the soil. Worm compost, mostly derived from vegetable waste, is also highly fertile. Liquid comfrey, which is a good source of nitrogen and phosphate, and seaweed extract, which contains trace elements, can be used throughout the growing season to boost growth.

If you test your soil and find that it is deficient in nutrients but you do not want to add a chemical formulation, choose from among

LEFT Growing different crops together, such as beetroot (beets) and carrots, can help to minimize the incidence of species-specific pests and diseases.

the following to counter the particular deficiency: bonemeal, blood, fish and bone, hoof and horn, pelleted chicken manure, seaweed meal, rock phosphate, organic potash, ground limestone or dolomitic limestone and gypsum.

GREEN MANURES

Practising crop rotation, which is a good idea whether your garden is organic or not, can mean that a section of the vegetable plot lies fallow for a season. Growing a green manure will both help maintain the structure of the soil and help to replace nutrients that have been lost to the previous crop. Grazing rye, for example, is useful for improving the structure of the soil, while clover can add to the soil's fertility by taking up nitrogen from the air. The green

manure is sown, allowed to grow and then simply dug back into the ground before it matures, where it decomposes, releasing the nutrients as it does so. Sowing a green manure is also a good way of preventing weeds from colonizing what would otherwise be bare soil.

BIOLOGICAL CONTROLS

Biological controls are increasingly used to control many common pests, although some are not suitable for outdoor use. Among the most useful is *Bacillus thuringiensis*, a bacterium that prevents caterpillars from eating, thereby effectively killing them. The bacterial spores, which produce a protein that is toxic to caterpillars, are sprayed on to the leaves of any vegetable that is susceptible to caterpillar damage. Its increasing use in genetically modified corn is, unfortunately, making it less effective in the US, where resistant varieties of pests have developed. It is still worth using in UK gardens, however.

An effective biological control is available for slugs, in the form of a nematode (a tiny parasite) which is watered into the ground, and kills slugs by drying up their slime organs. The soil temperature needs

ABOVE A "lacewing hotel" provides an area where lacewings – which prey on aphids, larvae, mites and thrips – can live.

to be above 5°C/41°F. The nematode is completely harmless to children, wildlife and pets, and birds and hedgehogs can safely eat slugs after application.

Biological controls usually work best when the weather is warm. Introduce them as soon as the first signs of attack are noticed. Be patient and accept that there will be some damage before the biological agent takes effect. When you use biological controls there will always be some pests, which are essential for the predator to continue to breed, but the population will be reduced.

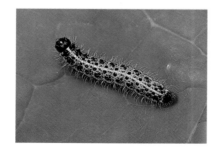

LEFT Biological controls can greatly reduce caterpillar damage.

cultivating
root
vegetables

Most root vegetables are easy to grow, and they will usually thrive in a range of conditions, as long as the ground is fertile, moist and weed-free. To avoid a build-up of pests and diseases in the soil, always practise crop rotation, making sure that you do not plant the same or related species in the same place in consecutive years. If you observe the few basic guidelines on the following pages, you will be rewarded with good harvests of flavourful, fresh crops for your kitchen.

Growing beetroot

Beetroot (beet) needs an open, sunny position. It will grow in heavy soils, but does best in light but fertile ones with a pH of 6.5–7.5. Use a plot that was manured for the previous crop or one into which manure was dug the previous autumn. Sow directly into the open soil into drills 1cm/½in deep and 20cm/8in apart. The seed should be station sown at 8cm/3in intervals or sown thinly and thinned to that distance after germination. Beetroot seed is slow to germinate, but it can be speeded up by soaking for an hour in warm water before sowing. Sow seed in early spring, once the soil is 7°C/45°F, and successionally at two-week intervals until early summer. An earlier sowing can be made under cloches.

Keep beetroot weed-free but avoid damaging them with a hoe. Keep them supplied with constant

ABOVE Harvest beetroot by pulling it by hand from the ground. In heavier soils a fork may be needed to loosen the roots.

moisture. It is important to avoid alternating dry and wet periods, or they may split.

HARVESTING AND STORAGE

Pull the young beetroot while they are still quite small. This will be about seven weeks after sowing. Continue to pull as required. You may need to use a fork to help

ease later crops or those in heavy soils from the ground. If possible, do not break the thin root at the bottom of the globe, because this will "bleed", causing the beetroot to lose a lot of its colour. For a similar reason do not cut off the leaves; twist them off, leaving about 5cm/2in on the beet.

Beetroot can be left in the ground until it is required, except in cold districts, where it can be lifted, cleaned and placed in trays of just-moist sand or peat substitute and stored in a cool, frost-free shed or garage.

PESTS AND DISEASES

Beetroot is reasonably trouble-free in terms of possible pests and diseases. Birds may eat the young seedlings when they first appear, so keep these off with netting of some sort. If any diseases occur, burn or dispose of the affected plants and re-sow them elsewhere.

LEFT Beetroot growing in a block in a raised bed. This method enables you to control the growing medium and grow crops unsuited to your soil.

Growing turnips

Turnips are a member of the brassica family and should be included with cabbages in a rotational sequence. They need an open, sunny situation and a light soil, with a pH of 6.0–7.0, although they can be grown in heavier soil. There must be plenty of organic material in the soil so that it does not dry out. The manure should be left from a previous crop or dug in the previous autumn.

Sow early varieties of turnip under cloches in late winter for early crops or in open ground from early spring. Sow seed in drills 1cm/½in deep and 23cm/9in apart. When the seedlings are big enough to handle, thin them to about 13cm/5in apart. Continue to sow at two- to three-week intervals for a continuous supply of small, tender turnips throughout the summer. For varieties to be harvested in autumn and winter, sow in midsummer. They should be at the same depth, but rows should be about 30cm/12in apart. Thin seedlings to 20cm/8in.

If you want to grow turnips just as "greens", sow thinly in late summer and there should be no need to thin. Rows can be as close as 8–10cm/3–4in.

The secret of growing good turnips is to keep them moist so that they can grow quickly. Keep them weeded.

HARVESTING AND STORAGE

Harvest the early and summer varieties as soon as they are the size of golf balls. Larger and older turnips become woody, so rather than sowing one long row, it is better to sow short rows at different times to provide a steady supply of young turnips. Varieties sown in midsummer can be harvested from autumn onwards as they are required. The "greens" can be harvested as young leaves from spring into summer.

Turnips can be left in the ground until they are required. In very cold areas or if they are likely to be frozen in the ground and impossible to extract, they can be lifted, the tops removed and the globes stored in trays of just-moist sand or peat substitute, and kept in a frost-free place.

ABOVE Turnips are an excellent crop to grow, as they can be harvested over a long period.

CULTIVATION

Summer
Sowing time: late winter (under cloches) to early spring
Sowing distance: thinly
Sowing depth: 1cm/½in
Distance between sown rows: 23cm/9in
Thinning distance: 13cm/5in
Harvesting: summer

Autumn and winter
Sowing time: mid- to late summer
Sowing distance: thinly
Sowing depth: 1cm/½in
Distance between sown rows: 30cm/12in
Thinning distance: 20cm/8in
Harvesting: autumn and winter

Greens
Sowing time: late summer
Sowing distance: thinly
Sowing depth: 1cm/½in
Distance between sown rows: 8–10cm/3–4in
Thinning distance: none
Harvesting: spring and early summer

PESTS AND DISEASES

Turnips suffer from cabbage root fly. Placing a collar of roofing felt around the plant's stem will prevent the adults from laying their eggs near the plant. Caterpillars are another problem. Cover the plants with netting or fleece to stop butterflies laying their eggs. You can remove caterpillars by hand, or use a biological or chemical spray – follow the manufacturer's instructions. Flea beetle, which is likely to be the worst pest, should be treated with derris dust. Diseases can include violet root rot and club root. Destroy any affected plants.

Growing swedes

Like most root crops, swedes (rutabagas or yellow turnips) prefer an open site and a light soil with a pH of 6.0–7.0, although they can be grown on heavier soils. As with most brassicas, the soil should not be too acid. Lime the soil if necessary to reduce the acidity. The ground should not be freshly manured, but it is important that it contains as much organic material as possible because the soil should be moisture-retentive. Add manure during autumn digging. Sow thinly in late spring or early summer into drills that are 38cm/15in apart and 1cm/½in deep. Thin the swedes to 23cm/9in apart, preferably doing this in stages. Make sure that the soil is kept moist throughout summer, otherwise any check in the growth may result in woody or split globes. Keep the weeds down.

HARVESTING AND STORAGE

Swedes can be harvested from autumn onwards, throughout the winter, once they are large enough to use. Lift the globes as they are required. In most soils they can simply be pulled from the soil, but in heavier ones they may need loosening with a fork first.

Swedes are completely hardy and can be left in the soil as long as necessary. Some varieties become woody if they are left in the ground until the end of winter, and these should be lifted and stored in trays of just-moist sand or peat substitute in a cool, frost-free shed or garage.

PESTS AND DISEASES

Being brassicas, swedes are prone to the same pests and diseases as the rest of the cabbage family, for example cabbage root fly and caterpillars. Flea beetles are a particular scourge, and the leaves should be dusted with derris as soon as they are spotted. Mildew can also be a problem, but there are now varieties that are resistant. Club root is another problem to look out for – any affected plants should be removed immediately and thrown away or destroyed.

> **CULTIVATION**
>
> Sowing time: late spring to early summer
> Sowing distance: thinly
> Sowing depth: 1cm/½in
> Distance between sown rows: 38cm/15in
> Thinning distance: 23cm/9in
> Harvesting: autumn onwards

LEFT Swedes have a long growing season and will grow best in cool, damp conditions.

Growing kohl rabi

Kohl rabi needs an open, sunny situation, preferably with light soil with a pH of 6.0–7.0, but it will grow on heavier ground. The soil should be well manured from an earlier crop or during the previous autumn. The seed should be sown thinly in drills, about 1cm/½in deep and 30cm/12in apart. Sowing can start under cloches in late winter for an early crop or in early spring in the open ground. Continue to sow at three-week intervals until late summer for a continuous crop of tender globes. Thin to 15cm/6in for earlier crops and to 20cm/8in for later ones. Watering is not as crucial as for turnips, but they are less likely to split if the moisture supply to the roots is constant. Keep weeded, but take care that you do not damage the roots with the hoe.

HARVESTING AND STORAGE

The stems are best harvested when they are about the size of tennis balls. Most varieties get rather woody after that. Later crops can be left in the ground until early winter and possibly even later in milder areas. They are very easy to harvest as they can be simply pulled from the ground. When harvesting, shorten the root and cut back the leaves, leaving short stems before taking them into the kitchen for preparation.

RIGHT The leaves of these healthy-looking kohl rabi are in perfect condition. These have been planted in a block.

There is usually no need to store kohl rabi, because they can be pulled from the ground as required. In colder areas the last crop can be pulled, cleaned and stored in trays of just-damp sand or peat substitute, but they do not keep as well as other root crops – they tend to shrivel.

PESTS AND DISEASES

Kohl rabi suffers from the same kind of pests and diseases as cabbage, including cabbage root fly and caterpillars. Flea beetles can be one of the worst pests, and leaves should be dusted with derris if an infestation occurs. Club root and mealy aphids can be a problem.

CULTIVATION

Sowing time: late winter (under cloches) and early spring to late summer
Sowing distance: thinly
Sowing depth: 1cm/½in
Distance between sown rows: 30cm/12in
Thinning distance: 15–20cm/6–8in
Harvesting: summer onwards

Growing carrots

Carrots are a cool-season crop, which will grow in fairly heavy soil, but they always do better in light ground, and sandy soils are perfect. Ideally, the soil pH should be between 6.5 and 7.5. Choose an open, sunny position, and make sure that the soil does not contain any large stones, which will make it impossible for the carrots to grow straight down. If the ground is particularly stony, make individual holes with a crowbar or similar implement, fill them with sieved compost and sow into these. Alternatively, sow into raised beds. Avoid freshly manured soil, which will cause the carrots to fork. Instead, either use an area of the vegetable garden that was manured for a previous crop, or apply the manure in the previous autumn so that it has time to break down over the winter months. Crops will benefit from the addition of a general fertilizer to the ground about a week before sowing and at a rate of about 50–75g/2–3oz per square metre/yard, but avoid adding too much nitrogen to the ground before sowing.

Most carrots do not transplant well and should be sown direct rather than being started under glass. Round-rooted cultivars can be raised under glass if the seed is sown in modules, and short-rooted forms can be started in biodegradable tubes and transplanted. Otherwise, sow seed for both early and maincrop carrots as thinly as possible in drills 1cm/½in deep and set 15–20cm/ 6–8in apart. Sow under cloches, a frame or a floating mulch in late winter or in the open from early spring, but not before the soil has warmed up to at least 7°C/45°F. Sow successively, with the last sowing in early summer.

When the seedlings appear, carefully thin the earlies to about 8cm/3in apart, to encourage rapid development, and maincrop varieties to 5–8cm/2–3in apart, depending on the size of carrots required. It is always best to thin on a muggy, windless evening in order to avoid attracting carrot flies, which are active on bright, sunny days and will scent the crushed or damaged foliage. For the same reason, remove all thinnings and bury them as deeply as possible in the compost heap.

SOWING WITH SAND

For best results carrots must be sown thinly, for both early and maincrop varieties. To help with this, mix the seed with a little silver sand and "sow" the mixture.

THINNING

Thin the carrots only if necessary. Do so on a still, muggy evening to prevent the smell of the carrots travelling and betraying their presence to carrot flies. Water after thinning.

HARVESTING

Shorter varieties can be pulled out by hand, but longer ones and those grown on heavier soils will need digging out with a fork. Try to avoid piercing the roots with the tines of the fork.

RIGHT A flourishing row of carrots, coming to maturity. These will be ready for harvesting a few at a time, whenever they are required for the kitchen.

Weed regularly but take care to avoid damaging the young carrots. A mulch of grass clippings between rows will help to keep down weeds and retain moisture in the soil. Water regularly, especially in dry weather.

HARVESTING AND STORAGE

Harvesting can begin at a very early stage as the thinnings can be delicious, although they are rather tedious to clean. Early carrots can be dug up from late spring onwards, approximately seven weeks after sowing. Maincrop carrots take a little longer and are ready from ten weeks onwards. Shorter varieties can be pulled, but longer ones and those that have been grown in heavier soils will need digging out with a fork.

Carrots are usually left in the ground until they are required. They may even be left in the ground over winter unless there are a lot of slugs or the winter is harsh. Instead, they can be lifted, cleaned and placed in a tray of just-moist sand or peat substitute.

PESTS AND DISEASES

The worst pest is undoubtedly carrot fly, the maggots of which burrow into the carrots. There are now some resistant varieties, such as 'Fly Away', and new ones are constantly being developed. Be careful when thinning, because the flies are attracted by smell, and the

bruising of any part of the carrot will release the tell-tale odour. Planting garlic nearby is a traditional way of disguising the smell. Another cumbersome but effective method is to erect a fine mesh barrier, 90cm/3ft high, around the carrots. This deflects the flies, which fly quite close to the ground.

STORING

1 Carrots, like most root crops, can be stored in trays of just-moist sand or peat substitute. Place a shallow layer of peat substitute in the bottom of a deep tray and then lay rows of carrots on top.

The principal disease from which carrots are likely to suffer is violet root rot, in which, as its name suggests, the root rots, becoming a violet colour. Burn or throw away all affected plants and make sure that you do not use the same ground for carrots for at least a couple of years.

2 Sprinkle a few handfuls of peat substitute over the carrots. Place another layer of carrots on top and cover these with more peat. Repeat with more layers until the tray is full, topping off with a final layer of peat.

Growing Jerusalem artichokes

Unlike most vegetables, Jerusalem artichokes are tolerant of light shade. They are also tolerant of a range of soils and will even grow in comparatively poor ones, although best results will be obtained from ground that has been manured during the previous autumn and has a pH of 6.0–7.5. Do not overfeed, because this may result in lush vegetation at the expense of tubers.

Jerusalem artichokes are best grown from tubers, rather than from seed. If you cannot find named varieties, tubers from the greengrocer can be used. Plant the tubers at any time in spring when the soil is workable, 10–13cm/4–5in deep, in holes made with a trowel.

They should be about 38cm/15in apart and the rows should be 90cm/3ft apart.

They need little attention apart from being kept weed-free. If they are likely to be rocked by the wind, draw earth up around the stems to help stabilize them so that the tubers are not disturbed. In very windy sites, individual stems may need to be supported with canes. The stems can be cut off in summer when they reach a height of about 1.8m/6ft to lessen the chance of wind damage; this is necessary not so much because the plants will be flattened but because the tubers will be disturbed by the movement of the plants and not develop properly.

CULTIVATION

Planting time: spring
Planting distance: 38cm/15in
Planting depth: 10–13cm/4–5in
Distance between rows: 90cm/
   3ft
Harvesting: summer onwards

HARVESTING AND STORAGE

The tubers can be lifted once the leaves start to wither in autumn. Cut off the stems, then lift the tubers with a fork, digging right under them. Sift through the soil to check that all the pieces are removed. Any piece of tuber remaining in the soil will grow again in the following year. This is not a problem if you plan to plant in the same place next year, but a nuisance if you do not. They can be difficult to eradicate, especially in heavy soils where it is easy to miss tubers, so harvest carefully.

Jerusalem artichokes are frost hardy and are best stored in the ground and dug only as they are required. A few can be dug if frost makes digging impossible, and stored in trays of just-moist sand or peat substitute in a frost-free shed or garage.

PESTS AND DISEASES

Jerusalem artichokes are not susceptible to pests and diseases.

LEFT Though the tubers are the only edible part of Jerusalem artichokes, the plants – which grow up to 1.8m/6ft high – produce attractive pointed leaves.

Growing radishes

Summer radishes should be grown in an open, sunny position. They do not need a deep, rich soil but prefer one that does not dry out or they will run to seed. The pH should be 6.5–7.5.

Sowing can start under cloches in late winter or in early spring in the open soil. Sow in shallow drills about 1cm/½in deep and 15cm/6in apart. Water the soil if it is dry at the time of sowing. Sow thinly so that little thinning is required, then thin to about 2.5cm/1in. Alternatively, sow seeds 2.5cm/1in apart, so they will not need thinning. You can make successional sowings every two weeks, which will give you a fresh supply over a long period.

Sow the larger winter radishes at about midsummer. Do not sow too early or they may run to seed. These should be sown in drills set 25cm/10in apart. When they are large enough to handle, thin to about 13cm/5in apart.

ABOVE Radishes are harvested simply by pulling them from the ground by hand when they are large enough to eat.

HARVESTING AND STORAGE

Summer radishes should be pulled when they are large enough to eat. Discard any that have become large or old because these will be too woody as well as too hot to eat. Winter radishes can be dug up from autumn onwards.

Summer radishes quickly shrivel once they are out of the ground and should be eaten as soon as possible. Long-rooted winter varieties can be left in the ground until they are required. If severe frosts are threatened, which would make digging them from the ground impossible, dig the roots and store them under cover in trays of just-moist peat substitute or sand.

PESTS AND DISEASES

Radishes suffer from the same pests and diseases as cabbages, including cabbage root fly and caterpillars. Flea beetle is likely to be the worst problem, and should beetles appear, young plants should be dusted with derris. Slugs are also partial to radishes and can leave unsightly holes in the roots. If anything worse than this happens, destroy the plants and re-sow elsewhere.

ABOVE These neat rows of radishes have been planted in abundance. You will have to consume large quantities to make use of so many at once, and radishes left in the ground for too long tend to be woody, so it is best to sow small quantities in succession.

Growing parsnips

Parsnips need an open, sunny position. They can be grown in heavy soils, but they prefer light ones, and the ideal pH is 6.5–7.0. They do best in a fertile soil, but freshly manured ground will cause them to fork, so grow them in an area that was manured for the previous crop, or dig in manure in the autumn. Always use fresh seed; old seed is unlikely to be viable. The seed should be station sown at 15–20cm/6–8in intervals in 1cm/½in drills. The rows should be 30cm/12in apart. Do not sow too early – the soil should be at least 7°C/45°F – but they do need a long growing season, so sow as soon as you can. Parsnips are slow to germinate, so sow a few radishes between the stations of parsnips. These will appear quickly and mark the line

ABOVE Station sow parsnips in groups of three. As soon as the seedlings are large enough to handle, remove the weakest two seedlings in each group.

of the rows, making it easier to hoe without accidentally disturbing the germinating parsnips.

In stony soils the parsnips may fork and produce stunted growth, rather than the desired conical shape. To avoid this, make holes with a crowbar at each sowing

station, moving it in a circle to make a conical hole in the ground. Fill the holes with any good growing medium and sow the seeds in this.

Thin the seeds to one to each station as soon as they are big enough to handle. Keep free from weeds. Water in dry spells because sudden rain after a prolonged dry spell may cause the roots to split. In cold climates cover the rows of parsnips with straw in winter.

CULTIVATION

Sowing time: early spring
Sowing distance: station sow at 15–20cm/6–8in
Sowing depth: 1cm/½in
Distance between sown rows: 30cm/12in
Harvesting: late autumn until spring

PLANTING IN STONY GROUND

1 At the required sowing intervals, make a conical hole with a crowbar.

2 Fill with a medium such as potting compost (soil mix) and sow in the centre, covering the seed with more compost.

RIGHT Parsnips can be left in the ground until they are required.

HARVESTING AND STORAGE

Parsnips can be harvested from autumn. Although they can be lifted before the leaves die back, most gardeners wait for this. Many gardeners also wait until after the first frosts, because these make parsnips taste sweeter. Dig the roots from the ground with a fork. In heavy soil or if the parsnips have deep roots, take care that the fork does not damage the flesh rather than lifting it out of the ground.

Parsnips are very hardy and should be left in the ground until they are required. If a frosty spell is forecast, however, it can be a good idea to lift a few while you can still get them out of the ground, and place them in trays of just-moist peat substitute or sand until they are required. They are a late crop and may be harvested in spring well beyond the time that the ground may be required for the next crops. The parsnips can be dug up and temporarily stored in sand or peat substitute.

PESTS AND DISEASES

Pale or brown patches on the leaves may indicate celery fly – destroy any affected leaves. Parsnips are also prone to carrot fly and canker, but there are some canker-resistant varieties.

LEFT Harvest parsnips by digging a fork well under the roots and carefully levering them out.

Growing potatoes

Potatoes will do best if they are grown in an open, sunny position. Because earlies are likely to emerge through the ground before the last of the frosts, try to choose a warm, protected spot away from frost pockets. They will grow on most soils, although they prefer slightly acid conditions, with a pH of 5.0–6.0. The soil should be fertile, but avoid planting potatoes into newly manured ground.

Earlies should be chitted. This involves standing the seed potatoes on a tray so that the eyes are facing upwards. Place the tray in a cool but frost-free place that is in good light although out of direct sunlight. Short shoots will appear, and these get the crop off to a good start. Maincrop can be treated in the same way, although it is not essential.

First earlies are planted in early spring, followed by second earlies two weeks later. Draw out a row with a hoe about 10cm/4in deep and place potatoes at 30cm/12in

intervals. Rows should be 45cm/18in apart. Alternatively, the potatoes can be planted in holes dug with a trowel or with a special potato planter. Whichever method you use, cover the potatoes with soil and then draw up more soil to form a low ridge above them. When the shoots reach heights of 23–25cm/9–10in, draw earth up around them along the rows to make certain that all the tubers are well covered; otherwise they turn green. Continue to do this until the foliage touches across the rows.

Second earlies and maincrop are treated in the same way, except that they are planted in the second half of spring and the potatoes are set 38cm/15in apart and in rows 60cm/24in apart for second earlies and 75cm/30in apart for maincrop.

Keep an eye on weather reports, and if frost is forecast cover any shoots with newspaper or horticultural fleece. Keep all potatoes, especially earlies, well

watered, particularly if there is a prolonged dry spell forecast.

An alternative method of growing potatoes is to plant them under a sheet of black plastic. Place the plastic sheet along the row and anchor it by burying the edges in the soil. Cut slits at the relevant intervals and plant potatoes through them.

HARVESTING AND STORAGE

Early potatoes are harvested in early summer, usually just as their flowers are opening, which should be about 12 weeks after planting. They are usually lifted as they are required. Maincrop are left in the soil until the autumn and are usually all lifted at once and stored.

CULTIVATION

First earlies
Planting time: early spring
Planting distance: 30cm/12in
Planting depth: 10–13cm/4–5in
Distance between rows:
    45cm/18in
Harvesting: early summer

Second earlies
Planting time: mid-spring
Planting distance: 38cm/15in
Planting depth: 10–13cm/4–5in
Distance between rows:
    60cm/24in
Harvesting: summer onwards

Maincrop
Planting time: mid- to late spring
Planting distance: 38cm/15in
Planting depth: 10–13cm/4–5in
Distance between rows:
    75cm/30in
Harvesting: autumn

CHITTING

Before planting, place the seed potatoes in a tray in a light place (but out of direct sunlight) in order to "chit". This means that the potatoes produce shoots.

PLANTING

Hoe out a trench 10cm/4in deep and lay the tubers about 30–38cm/12–15in apart, depending on the type. Cover with soil and earth (hill) up into a low ridge.

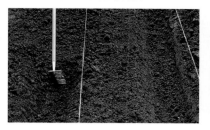  

1 Use a draw hoe, spade or rake head to make wide, flat-bottomed or V-shaped drills 10–13cm/4–5in deep. Space the rows about 45cm/18in apart for early varieties, 60cm/24in for second earlies, and 75cm/30in for the maincrop.

2 Space the tubers about 30–38cm/ 12–15in apart in the rows. Make sure that the shoots or eyes (buds about to grow into shoots) face upwards. For larger tubers, leave only three sprouts on each one and rub off the others.

3 Carefully cover the tubers by pulling the excavated soil back into the drill. Potatoes must be earthed (hilled) up as they grow to prevent the tubers from turning green and to protect the shoots from frost damage.

To harvest earlies, dig a fork in well below the potatoes and lever them out of the soil, at the same time pulling on the haulm (stems and leaves). For maincrop potatoes, remove the haulm about two weeks before harvesting so that the skins on the tubers harden. Lift the maincrop on a dry, warm day and leave them lying in the sun for an hour or two to let them dry and to harden the skins.

Do not leave potatoes in the light for too long. Pack them into hessian (burlap) or paper sacks and store them in a dark, cool but frost-free place. Alternatively, they can be stored in trays as long as no light gets to the tubers. Regularly check all potatoes and remove any that have started to rot.

PESTS AND DISEASES

The worst problem that can occur is blight, which is particularly prevalent in wet years. The leaves go yellow and brown and start to curl. Eventually the haulm may fall to pieces. The potatoes develop black patches, which eventually turn into a slimy, evil-smelling rot. Do not plant potatoes on ground that was affected the year before (either from potato or tomato blight). Earth (hill) plants up well to keep the spores from the tubers. If necessary, spray with the appropriate copper-based fungicide, in wet years preferably before blight appears. Look out for resistant varieties. Another common disease is potato scab, which disfigures the surface of

PLANTING UNDER A PLASTIC SHEET

1 If you do not want the effort of earthing (hilling) up, plant potatoes under a black plastic sheet. Bury the edges securely in the soil.

2 Use a sharp knife to make rows of cross-shaped slits in the plastic where the tubers are to be planted. Space the slits according to the type of potato.

3 Plant the tubers through the slits, using a trowel. Make sure that each tuber is covered with 10–12cm/4–5in of soil. The shoots will grow through the slits.

the tubers. To avoid it occurring, do not grow potatoes on ground that has been recently limed or manured. Other diseases include spraing, violet root rot and blackleg.

The main pests are slugs and wireworms, both of which eat holes in the tubers. Other pests can include cutworms and potato cyst eelworms.

ABOVE This row of potatoes shows the earth drawn up around the stems. If light is allowed to reach the tubers, they will turn green, showing the presence of poisonous solanines.

EARTHING UP

When the potato shoots reach 23–25cm/ 9–10in long, draw the soil up around them along the rows. As the plants continue to grow, repeat the process of earthing (hilling) up.

FROST PROTECTION

Once the potato shoots have emerged through the soil, they will need protecting from possible frost damage. Cover them over with horticultural fleece or even with newspaper.

HARVESTING

To harvest, dig a fork well under the potatoes and draw it up through the soil, bringing the tubers up with the earth. Take care that you do not damage the tubers on the tines of the fork.

Growing salsify and scorzonera

Choose a site that is sunny and open. As with most root crops, both salsify and scorzonera like a light, deep soil with a pH of 6.0–7.5, although they will grow in heavier conditions. The soil should be deeply dug and have organic matter added well in advance of sowing because they do not like freshly manured ground. To be sure of having a sufficiently large crop, both must be sown as early as possible to give a long growing season, although scorzonera should not be sown too early or it will run to seed. Seed should be sown by mid-spring, 1cm/½in deep in drills set 25cm/10in apart. Use fresh seed rather than any left from a previous season. Thin the seedlings to 15cm/6in apart. Although they can be grown closer together, they are more difficult to dig up individually.

Neither salsify nor scorzonera needs a great deal of attention from the gardener, apart from being kept weeded. Take care that you do not damage the roots with a hoe, because this will cause them to bleed. On the whole, they will not require watering, although if there is a prolonged drought, you should give them a good soaking once a week. A mulch will both keep down weeds and conserve the necessary moisture in the soil.

RIGHT Producing a healthy crop of salsify is not difficult, as it is a robust plant, and it deserves to be grown more widely.

HARVESTING AND STORAGE

Like parsnips, salsify and scorzonera taste best after they have experienced a frost. This is not to say that you cannot harvest earlier, and they are usually ready from mid-autumn onwards. Dig the roots up with a fork as required, taking care not to bruise or damage them. Salsify should be harvested and used during the first winter because it is a biennial. Scorzonera, however, is a perennial and can be left in the ground and harvested in the following autumn and winter, which gives the roots the chance to get larger.

Both plants are very hardy and can be left in the ground until needed, although it can be a good idea to lift a few and store them in trays of just-moist sand if a hard frost is forecast, because it may then be difficult to get them out of the ground.

PESTS AND DISEASES

Neither salsify nor scorzonera tends to suffer from pests or diseases.

CULTIVATION

Sowing time: early to mid-spring
Sowing distance: thinly
Sowing depth: 1cm/½in
Distance between sown rows: 25cm/10in
Thinning distance: 15cm/6in
Harvesting: autumn and winter

Index

The publisher would like to thank *Garden World Images* for supplying the pictures on pages 30b, 31tl, 52 and 56.